For Eric, Jael, Noel, and Ezra,
my dearest prayer partners in every good work.
I'm ever grateful for you.

YOU

ARE

REDEEMED

——

NANA DOLCE

DEVOTIONS FOR LIVING A WHOLE NEW LIFE

New Growth Press, Greensboro, NC 27401
Newgrowthpress.com
Copyright © 2024 Nana Dolce

Cover Design and Interior Design: Cary Bates

ISBN: 978-1-64507-483-0 (paperback)
ISBN: 978-1-64507-484-7 (ebook)

Library of Congress Cataloging-in-Publication Data

Names: Dolce, Nana, 1981- author.
Title: You are redeemed : devotions for living a whole new life / Nana
  Dolce.
Description: Greensboro, NC : New Growth Press, [2024] | Series: Gospel
  truth for women
Identifiers: LCCN 2024021014 (print) | LCCN 2024021015 (ebook) | ISBN
  9781645074830 (print) | ISBN 9781645074847 (ebook)
Subjects: LCSH: Bible. Exodus--Criticism, interpretation, etc. | Devotional
  calendars.
Classification: LCC BS1245.52 .D56 2024 (print) | LCC BS1245.52 (ebook) |
  DDC 242--dc23/eng/20241101
LC record available at https://lccn.loc.gov/2024021014
LC ebook record available at https://lccn.loc.gov/2024021015

Printed in India

32 31 30 29 28 27 26 25   1 2 3 4 5

CONTENTS

Introduction

We are the new covenant people of God—women redeemed from the bondage of sin and death. This is true, and yet the full experience of our redemption is still to come. We live now in a dark world with diseases, distress, and distractions. We have discouraged family and friends around us. And sometimes we feel overwhelmed and a bit lonely ourselves. What does God's abiding presence mean in moments of pain? Does he sympathize with us? Where is true rest in a world of stress and suffering? How do we know we will persevere to the very end? These are good questions, and our redemption in Christ speaks to each one!

You Are Redeemed: Devotions for Living a Whole New Life will guide you on an eight-week journey through the book of Exodus. Its purpose is to assure you of this central truth: the God who redeemed you for himself is sustaining and preparing you for a glorious eternal home with him.

God didn't rescue the Israelites from bondage for the sake of their freedom alone. Yes, their liberation from ruthless Pharaoh was a vital part of God's work of redemption. Yet his purposes were higher than that. God delivered Israel for *himself*. He drew near to make himself known. God designed a tent for himself among the Israelites and guided them across the wilderness by his mighty hand. God gave his people laws to reflect his own holiness. And he provided a mediator to teach them his ways. Yahweh moved from being a seemingly remote deity in Israel's eyes to the covenant Lord God who tabernacled among them. God erected a sanctuary—a symbol of his heavenly temple—amid his people. This astounding second book of the Bible reminds us of God's intentions, shown since the opening pages of Scripture.

God created human beings to know and dwell with him. Sin separated Adam and Eve and all their children (including us) from God, but the Creator never abandoned his original plan. The book of Exodus inches forward toward a new kind of Eden. God comes to reveal himself more fully to Israel and to tabernacle with his people. Exodus marks a remarkable place in redemptive history. Yet the book begs for something greater.

Access to God's presence during the book of Exodus is awesome, but it also presents a temporary system with strictly defined roles and boundaries. Simply put, certain people can approach God on specific occasions, and often at a distance. The reader can't help but wonder, *Is this as good as it gets? Is this restricted followership on Mount Sinai the closest God's people will ever get to their Redeemer?* Friend, the gospel gives an emphatic NO to that question! What began in Exodus has its complete fulfillment in Jesus Christ—the Son of God who came in the flesh to dwell with humanity and is preparing a place in God's heavenly house for his church (John 14:1–3). Sister, in this Christ, you are welcomed—not to Mount Sinai, but to Mount Zion (Hebrews 12:18–24)!

God will gather his countless children to communion with him forever. He is working at this very moment to get you ready for a wondrous eternity. He is sustaining you in a kingdom that has come—and yet is still ahead. You are a woman journeying through an earthly (often pain-filled) wilderness to a promised heavenly home. *You Are Redeemed* is written to focus your attention on the God who travels with you. This is an eight-week, forty-day devotional. A forty-day devotional in the book of Exodus is only fitting. May these days assure you of the truths that your God

- remembers,
- redeems,
- provides,
- covenants,
- reveals,
- judges and restores,
- prepares, and
- dwells with his people.

Sister, you were redeemed for God himself. So together let's learn to live each day— whether it brings sunshine or rain—in view of that glorious reality!

God Remembers

This week's readings reveal the living God who remembers his promises. God remembers captive Israel as she groans in slavery. He sends words and signs to comfort and reassure her. We are God's redeemed people. We are living in a world of pain and sorrow while awaiting the full experience of our redemption. As we wait, know that God has given his Word and the ultimate sign—the resurrection of his Son—to comfort us. Sister, even in times of difficulty, trust that God remembers you!

EXODUS 1-6

READ

Exodus 1

The midwives in this story, Shiphrah and Puah, had a fear of God that was greater than their fear of Pharaoh. What do you fear?

How might a greater fear of God help defeat these fears?

I remember the day I first heard of Leah Sharibu—a young woman standing her ground before terrorists. Here's her story:[1]

On February 19, 2018, 110 teenage girls (all students at a boarding school in northeast Nigeria) were kidnapped by Boko Haram, a faction of the terrorist group known as the Islamic State of West Africa Province. Five of the girls died while in captivity. Boko Haram released the remaining girls a month later—that is, all except Leah Sharibu.

Leah, a Christian girl who was fourteen at the time of her capture, is the only student from the school still held hostage today. According to the testimony of her classmates, Leah was given permission to return to her parents along with the other girls. However, her release had one condition: convert to Islam first. Leah refused. She wouldn't comply with her captor's demand to abandon her Christian faith. For this, the teen has remained in captivity since 2018. Boko Haram has threatened to make Leah their slave for life.

Leah Sharibu shows us that not all fears are equal. Her fear (reverent awe) of God prevails above her fear of Boko Haram. The girl is imprisoned by terrorists who hold no true power over her because of her reverence for Someone greater. Young Leah reminds me of the Hebrew midwives in Exodus 1.

Shiphrah and Puah were enslaved midwives living in Egypt. They assisted Israelite mothers in labor and delivery. The two women must have been busy—after all, Israel was experiencing a baby boom. God's promise to make Abraham into a great nation was proving true in Egypt (Genesis 12:1-3). The Israelites multiplied, but as their numbers grew so did Pharaoh's worries.

Shiphrah and Puah lived under the rule of a crafty pharaoh. The man wore a crown with a raised serpent attached, and just like a snake, he was determined to swallow Israel. He worked to subdue Israel's population with ruthless enslavement and hard labor. But who can override God's purposes? The more Pharaoh oppressed the Israelites, the more babies Shiphrah and Puah caught. The midwives were eventually summoned by Pharaoh and told, "When you serve as midwife to the Hebrew women and see them on the birthstool, if it is a son, you shall kill him, but if it is a daughter, she shall live" (Exodus 1:16).

Pharaoh ordered these midwives to bring death instead of life. These lowly women should have feared Pharaoh, and likely they were afraid. Yet Pharaoh held no ultimate power over them because they feared a King on a higher throne. To fear God is to revere him—to regard his unmatched supremacy, holiness, and faithfulness with awe, adoration, trust, and worship. The midwives honored God by defying Pharaoh, and *they* multiplied also as God gave them families.

Sister, the fears you and I will encounter today won't compare to Shiphrah's and Puah's or to Leah Sharibu's. But consider this: if fearing God could free *these* humble women from the terror of genocidal rulers and terrorists, then surely our reverence for God can crush our lesser fears! Shiphrah, Puah, and Leah are worthy examples—yet we have an even better one in Jesus. The threat of death held no power over him who delighted perfectly in the fear of the Lord (Isaiah 11:1-3). Friend, Jesus is your hope when threatened by fear. He has redeemed you from fear to revere *him* above all.

CONSIDER

▌ What does fear of man look like in your life? Who or what are you tempted to fear above God?

....
....
....
....

▌ How can fear lead us into sin? How can a reverential fear of God help defeat other fears?

....
....
....
....

▌ How can Christians best support persecuted brothers and sisters like Leah Sharibu?
Pray for Leah's perseverance, encouragement, and release from Boko Haram.

....
....
....
....

BELIEVE

But the midwives feared God and did not do as the king of Egypt commanded them, but let the male children live…. So God dealt well with the midwives. And the people multiplied and grew very strong. And because the midwives feared God, he gave them families.

EXODUS 1:17, 20–21

READ

Exodus 2

IDENTIFY

Enslaved Israel cried to a God who heard, remembered, and knew her sufferings. Do you believe that Jesus knows and sympathizes with your pain today?

How can this truth encourage your bold prayers?

It's a gift it is to feel heard, seen, and known—especially in a time of suffering. Rob Delaney would agree. Delaney is a writer and comedian. He's a funny guy, but his most recent work centers on the heavy topic of death. Delaney has buried two precious members of his family in the last few years. His bereavement has taught him the value of empathy.

Delaney's brother-in-law died by suicide while the comedian's two-year-old son was receiving cancer treatment. His son died shortly afterward. The trauma of these passings has altered Delaney. He reports being most at ease today "around people who've been through horrific tragedy."[2] His widowed sister is among that group. Delaney describes their bond in this way: "So my sister and I were hit by operatic levels of tragedy. . . . We now have a common language of grief and love and support . . . . we have a very special relationship now."[3]

Delaney's astounding loss is unique, and yet we can relate to him on the value of empathy. There's something special that happens when we sit across from someone who has walked the road we are on. That person brings a "knowing" to the conversation that frees us to be more of ourselves with them. And feeling free with another who hears, sees, and understands you is a blessing. Exodus 2:23-25 says that God "heard, saw, and knew" Israel's pain.

The pharaoh who ordered the death of the Israelite baby boys was dead, yet his oppression lived on. Israel groaned under the weight of her long enslavement, and the nation's cries went up to God. God remembered his covenant promises to Abraham and his children—to make Israel a fertile nation, planted in her own soil (Genesis 12:1-3). Exodus 2:23-25 emphasizes God's faithfulness to his covenant promises. And the narrator makes this point with interesting verbs. The passage ends like this: "God saw the people of Israel—and God knew" (Exodus 2:25). Unlike the dead pharaoh, Israel's covenant God was alive and ruling the world. He heard, remembered, saw, and *knew* their pain.

We have a knowing friend in Jesus. He became flesh and walked the road you're on—without sinning. Hebrews 2:17 explains that Jesus "had to be like his brothers and sisters in every way, so that he could become a merciful and faithful high priest in matters pertaining to God, to make atonement for the sins of the people" (CSB).

Our living Redeemer is a merciful and knowing High Priest (Hebrews 4:15). He experienced physical pain, rejection, betrayal, and bereavement. Jesus can even sympathize when your fervent prayers return to you with a divine no. He faced the horrors of the cross and drank the bitter cup of divine wrath, despite his pleas in the garden (Luke 22:42). Jesus suffered operatic levels of tragedy for the sake of our redemption.

Sister, our Redeemer is a High Priest who knows our language of grief. In Jesus, we have a Brother who hears, sees, and understands our sorrows. But even better, this Brother has become the fulfillment of every covenant promise of God. He can sustain you in those promises no matter what your present pain. So draw near to sit across from him in prayer today—he understands.

CONSIDER

▶ How have you been encouraged by the empathetic presence of another at a difficult time?

▶ How does God's knowing presence abide with Israel in her Egyptian captivity?

▶ Do you believe that Jesus can sympathize with your pain? How can this truth change your prayers to him today?

BELIEVE

For we do not have a high priest who is unable to sympathize with our weaknesses, but one who in every respect has been tempted as we are, yet without sin.

HEBREWS 4:15

READ

Exodus 3

IDENTIFY

Jesus promises to be with you always. Do you believe his promise?

How can trust in his words shape your perspective on your life today?

November 3, 2022, is forever stamped on my heart. That was the day my husband and I became the adoptive parents of our nineteen-month-old foster son. I am the mom to a toddler now, which means watching many episodes of *Sesame Street*. Elmo, a character on that show, is a major star at our house. And listening to Elmo speak has reminded me of the importance of pronouns.

Pronouns replace nouns when we're speaking or writing to prevent strange and unnecessary repetitions. For example, I substitute my first name "Nana" with the pronoun "I" to avoid referring to my name continuously in conversation. It sounds minor, and yet pronouns grow in sudden importance when you hear a character like Elmo speak. The personal pronoun "I" doesn't exist in Elmo's vocabulary—he calls himself "Elmo" and nothing else.

Even in Scripture, pronouns are essential. An important pronoun shows up today in Exodus 3:10–12, and it comes with great encouragement.

Moses was a baby saved from the genocidal pharaoh of Exodus 1–2. He is now a man tending sheep on Mount Horeb (also called Sinai) when a burning bush calls his attention and then his name. The angel of the Lord appeared to Moses in the flames and spoke. Israel's covenant God had seen the affliction and heard the cries of his oppressed people. He was going to free them from the Egyptians, and he was calling Moses to go to Pharaoh to mediate Israel's deliverance. Moses responded to this news with an immediate objection: "Who am I that I should go to Pharaoh and bring the children of Israel out of Egypt?" (v. 11). God's answer should have settled all reluctances: "But I will be with you" (v. 12). The noun behind a pronoun makes all the difference!

There's a scene in Matthew 28:16–20 that reminds me of Exodus 3:10–12. Jesus has risen from the grave. He directs his disciples up a mountain and appears to them with a commission: "Go therefore and make disciples of all nations, baptizing them in the name of the Father and of the Son and of the Holy Spirit, teaching them to observe all that I have commanded you" (vv. 19–20). Jesus's followers would go everywhere his authority reaches—the entire world—to multiply disciples. The Lord ends his charge with this comfort: "And behold, I am with you always, to the end of the age."

You and I belong to those commissioned by Christ to make disciples. Perhaps, like Moses on Mount Sinai, there are days you feel inadequate for this task. You think, *Who am I for such a task*? Evangelism can be a nerve-racking experience, and our attempts to teach the Bible can appear ineffective in our own eyes. Yet Jesus says, "I am with you always," which is our courage and hope.

Sometimes God sends us to faraway places. At other times, he brings far-off people to us. My hands are filled with the good work of evangelizing and discipling an Elmo-loving toddler. Whatever your assignment might be, you can persevere boldly in your gospel work for Christ. *He* is with you—and the noun behind a pronoun makes all the difference!

"And behold,
I am with
you always,
to the end
of the age."

MATTHEW 28:20

CONSIDER

▶ God encourages a hesitant Moses with the promise of his presence. How does Jesus do the same for you?

....

....

....

▶ How are you participating in Jesus's Great Commission? Where (or to whom) has the Lord sent you to teach and disciple?

....

....

....

▶ When have you experienced Jesus's presence during evangelism? Pray for the grace to believe that he is with you always—especially as you share and teach his Word to others!

....

....

....

BELIEVE

"Go therefore and make disciples of all nations, baptizing them in the name of the Father and of the Son and of the Holy Spirit, teaching them to observe all that I have commanded you. And behold, I am with you always, to the end of the age."

MATTHEW 28:19-20

READ
Exodus 4

IDENTIFY

Have you ever asked God for a sign that he is with you? God gave Moses signs to help convince the Israelites that God had taken note of their distress and would free them. They met these signs with belief and worship. But what sign do *we* have? The greatest sign of hope God has ever sent his people is the resurrection of his Son.

What difference should Jesus's resurrection make in your life today?

How can you greet this sign with belief and worship?

I learned to drive later than many people. I attended driving school post-college and purchased my first car just before I received my license. I remember learning all the traffic signs involved for passing the written portion of a driver's test. It seemed I had missed a lot as a passenger—many of these signs were new to me. But studying them made one thing clear: traffic signs demand a decision. Whatever its purpose—whether regulation (like a stop sign), warning (like a railroad crossing sign), or guidance (like a highway exit sign)—a road sign will ask for the attention and response of the driver. The same is true for the signs God sends to his people.

In Exodus 4, Moses journeys back to Egypt. His brother Aaron meets him in the wilderness, and together, they go to the Israelites with a staggering message: the God of their fathers has heard and seen their affliction and has come to free them from their oppression. I wonder how this news struck the ears of the disheartened Israelites. Likely, some believed while others doubted. But God had sent Moses to Israel with both words *and* signs for their assurance.

Moses came armed with three signs: (a) Moses's staff would turn into a serpent and then back into a staff; (b) his hand would come out of his cloak leprous and then emerge healed; and (c) water from the Nile would turn into blood on the dry ground. God enabled these early signs to verify Moses's words to Israel—not to Pharaoh. The God of their fathers had indeed come to redeem them from Egypt. "*Aaron spoke all the words that the LORD had spoken to Moses and did the signs in the sight of the people*" (v. 30). How would Israel respond? By God's grace, "*the people believed . . . [and] they bowed their heads and worshiped*" (v. 31, emphasis added).

We are God's redeemed people awaiting the full experience of our redemption in a world of disasters, distractions, and doubts. We are easily discouraged by our own sins, not to mention the atrocities of our fallen world. Yet, right now, God is making all things new. And the certainty of that coming restoration is seen in his Word and rests in his ultimate "sign"—the resurrection of his Son.

Easter Sunday has just passed as I write these words. Friend, if our daily enthusiasm for Jesus's resurrection matched our Easter Sunday excitement, it wouldn't be an overreaction, but only what's appropriate. Like a sign pointing a driver to her ultimate destination, the resurrection of Jesus Christ shouts of the future. A dead Jesus rose bodily from the grave, defeating sin, death, and all effects of the fall. A great reversal has occurred. History is moving toward the restoration of all creation and the glorification of those in Christ (Romans 8:21–25). Sister, our full and complete redemption is coming. Do you believe this?

The best sign God ever sent his covenant people was the resurrection of his Son, Jesus Christ. It's a sign that demands attention and response, for it authenticates every word and work of Christ—and it's the beginning of a coming harvest. Sister, let's receive God's Word and the sign of the resurrection with belief and worship. A dead Jesus rose bodily from the grave—worship today! Hallelujah, hallelujah!

CONSIDER

▶ How does Israel respond to God's word and signs? How do these transform a discouraged nation?

_____

_____

_____

_____

▶ How does the resurrection of Jesus Christ signify our full and complete redemption?

_____

_____

_____

_____

▶ A dead Jesus rose bodily from the grave! Do you believe this? Pray that the reality of the resurrection will anchor your hope for the future and encourage you today.

_____

_____

_____

_____

_____

BELIEVE

And the people believed; and when they heard that the LORD had visited the people of Israel and that he had seen their affliction, they bowed their heads and worshiped.

EXODUS 4:31

READ

Exodus 6

IDENTIFY

God comforts Israel by reminding her of his name. He's *Yahweh*, the covenant-keeping God who redeems. How is God's faithfulness a comfort to you in times of trouble?

I recently read a BBC article on the topic of my name—Nana.[4] The piece reported on developing legislation in Ghana—my birth country. It appears that the birth registry department of Ghana might refuse certain names it deems improper. "Nana" is among these names.

The article explained the situation this way: while "Nana" is a very popular unisex name in Ghana, it is technically a title of honor for Ghanaian chiefs and royals. In fact, to say "Nana" in the Akan language of Ghana is to say something equivalent to "Your Royal Highness." It seems the country's birth registry department wants to discourage modern parents from bestowing this high title on their children. We will see whether or not they are successful.

While most people don't have names equivalent to royal titles, a person's name is rarely "just a name." Whatever the culture, we give our children meaningful names we hope they will grow to embody in some capacity. This is what my parents intended with the name "Nana." They wanted a daughter whose manner would show the wisdom and influence of a noble sovereign. It's a nice wish, but one I cannot faithfully fulfill. In truth, only God perfectly embodies the splendor of his name.

God reminds Israel of his covenant name in our passage today. The nation that greeted God's word and signs with belief and worship yesterday is now discouraged and broken in spirit. Pharaoh didn't respond to God with the same awe. On the contrary, God's command to release his people only emboldened Pharaoh's ruthlessness. He forced the Israelites to meet their daily quota of bricks without the provision of straw (Exodus 5:10–23). Israel's faith buckled under the weight of the added oppression, and their worship turned to bitter complaint. Here, God shows up to declare his name.

God comforts Israel by reminding her of his name: "God spoke to Moses and said to him, 'I am the Lord'" (Exodus 6:2). This was the name given to Moses at the burning bush (Exodus 3:13–15). This was *Yahweh*, the I Am, the Lord who remembered and would keep every covenant promise made to Israel's forefathers. He is the God who remains unchanging and perfect in his character. God's revealed name testifies to his faithfulness, which had to be Israel's hope and comfort. God *would* redeem them!

Of course, the ultimate redemption the Lord planned from the beginning would stretch from enslaved Israel to reach all of his captive sons and daughters. Yahweh would reveal himself most clearly through his Son—Jesus Christ. Jesus shocked the Jews of his day by referring to himself as "I Am" (John 8:58). In him, we behold the eternal God whose faithfulness is unchanging. This Jesus would die and rise to set all his captive people free. He is the "I Am"—the covenant-keeping God of our redemption. King Jesus is the only sovereign who lives up to his name! May his faithfulness be your comfort today.

▶ Why does God remind mournful Israel of his name? Why should this comfort them?

_____

_____

_____

▶ How is Yahweh's covenant-keeping faithfulness most clearly revealed in Christ?

_____

_____

_____

▶ How is God's faithfulness a comfort to you in times of trouble? Pray for grace to always remember his unfailing faithfulness.

_____

_____

_____

BELIEVE

Jesus said to them, "Truly, truly, I say to you, before Abraham was, I am."

JOHN 8:58

Take & Share

The people who worshipped yesterday are broken in spirit today. Isn't that often our story? God comforts Israel by reminding her of his name. Yahweh is the covenant-keeping God who redeems. God's revealed name testifies to his faithfulness, and this is Israel's hope and comfort. The God of Israel has revealed himself more fully to us in his Son Jesus, the I AM. If yesterday's joys have become today's sorrows, find hope and comfort in Jesus—the covenant-keeping God of our redemption! Who do you know who needs to hear this word of comfort and hope? Share this truth with one other person.

God Redeems

This week's readings reveal a God who is redeeming a diverse people from all the families of the earth. The blood of Christ, the Lamb of God, has saved us from our sins and transferred us from darkness to the kingdom of light. Tests and temptations abound, and still we are redeemed and empowered by God's Spirit to live a new life of faith. Sister, *this* is the good news Christians sing of and proclaim to everyone they meet!

EXODUS 7 - 15:21

READ
Exodus 9

God's plan is to gather a diverse people to himself. How often do you pray for this to happen in the church?

Do you pray for this in your own personal relationships?

Some astronauts experience a dramatic shift in perspective as they gaze on the Earth from the cosmos. This phenomenon is called the "overview effect." The term was coined by Frank White, the space philosopher. White interviewed numerous astronauts and heard a similar story: from the distance of space, our vast, diverse, and fragmented planet is undeniably small, uniform, and whole. White said it this way on NASA's *Houston, We Have a Podcast*:

> The first thing that most people think about when they think about the overview effect is no borders or boundaries on the Earth. And we know that. But we create maps that show borders and boundaries. And what the astronauts were telling me was . . . I knew before I went into orbit, or went to the moon, that there weren't any little dotted lines. But it's knowing intellectually versus experiencing it.[1]

After seeing our planet from the window of the stars, many astronauts reenter Earth with an altered vision of a singular humanity. God is kind to give these men and women such a privileged perspective—whether in space or on land, it's a blessing to see things from a broader angle.

The Lord comes to Pharaoh in today's passage to offer a wider lens on the Egyptian plagues: God had all the families of the earth in view.

Yahweh promised to redeem Israel from slavery in Exodus 6:6. Today, we find that his acts of judgment against Egypt have begun. There are seven plagues between Exodus 7 and 9. The Nile River becomes blood; frogs, gnats, and flies each torment the land; death strikes Egypt's livestock; and boils fester on the skin of the Egyptian people. God's hand is heavy against Egypt, yet the callous Pharaoh refuses to let Israel go. So God sends a seventh plague of deadly hail, and a message with it.

God offers a stunning new perspective on the plagues. He sends Moses to explain his greater purpose behind these acts of judgment. God says to Pharaoh, "I have raised you up, to show you my power, so that my name may be proclaimed in all the earth" (9:16). The Egyptian plagues were sent to deliver Israel from slavery, but God didn't see Israel alone; he acted to reveal his power to various nations—the Israelites, the Egyptians, and all the earth. God uses his works of judgment and salvation to draw the nations of the earth to himself. His church today is a case in point.

The Bible tells a story of a great reversal. What was broken is made whole, and fragmented parts are united in the risen Christ. The church is a sign of this truth; diverse sinners across humanity will dwell together in sinless unity one day. Our churches are polarized today and still the reality of our one union in Christ stands. Our neighbors should experience an "overview effect" as they witness very different people communing together as one in the church.

Friend, God's plan in redemptive history has always been to gather a diverse and unified people to himself. How often do you pray for this reality to reflect across the church and within your own personal relationships? If we are honest, we can admit that this is hard to live out. As Irwyn Ince points out, "The pursuit [for unity in the church] is too hard. It is too perplexing, and often too painful, if our commitment is not drenched in the beautiful truth that we are participating in the beautiful plan and purpose of our beautiful God."[2] Let's ask God to turn our eyes to the beautiful truth of his plan for redeeming people from every tribe and nation— so we can pray that it will be so in our Christian community.

CONSIDER

▶ How does Exodus 9:16 alter your view of the Egyptian plagues? What was God's wider purpose for these acts of judgment?

....

....

....

....

▶ How has Jesus accomplished God's plan to gather the nations of the world to himself (see Matthew 28:18–19 and Acts 2:5–41)?

....

....

....

....

▶ Pray that God would help our churches (and our own friendships) to reflect our coming perfect unity in Christ!

....

....

....

....

BELIEVE

But for this purpose I have raised you up, to show you my power, so that my name may be proclaimed in all the earth.

EXODUS 9:16

Exodus 10

IDENTIFY

Exodus 10 is a picture of the darkness that fills the lives of those who turn from God. Many of us are surrounded by people living in great darkness. But those transferred from the domain of darkness into the kingdom of light are filled with the light of God's love. How can we learn to live in a dark world and still shine with Christ's love?

I remember the day I had to walk into a dark house by myself as a child. I lived in Accra, Ghana. A power outage in my developing neighborhood meant a fixed darkness that encircled me like a weighted blanket. I needed shoes to leave our compound (the fenced and gated area where our house sat) and a pair of slippers waited under my bed in a very dark house. Reaching them took Spirit-enabled courage!

Maybe you're not afraid of the dark, and still, like me, you would prefer to avoid it. Yet it's not always possible to escape the dark. Our days on this earth come with moments of physical darkness—and spiritual darkness. The truth is that you don't need a power outage to experience deep darkness. Many among us live in spiritual darkness—no matter how bright their lives may seem. Moses writes to convey this point in our passage today. God exposes Pharaoh's dark blindness and distinguishes between those who dwell in his light and those who do not.

God sent a seventh plague of hail to destroy the fields of Egypt. He followed this with locusts in the eighth plague, which devoured everything left by the hail. This threat of hunger seemed to budge Pharaoh's heart a bit. Perhaps this God he had considered a nobody in Exodus 5:2 was worth regarding after all? Pharaoh, with the urging of his people, agreed to meet God's demands halfway. He would temporarily release a portion of the Israelites—only the men could go and serve the Lord, no one else (Exodus 10:8–11).

Pharaoh had witnessed the sovereign power of a God like none other, and he still refused to surrender to this God with complete obedience. For this, Yahweh would crush Amon-Ra, the Egyptian chief god who personified the sun.[3] God would shroud the Egyptians in pitch darkness for three days but bathe the Israelites in light.

Friends, in Exodus 10:21-23, we catch a glimpse of all humanity and the two groups it represents. Everyone you meet, regardless of their background, walks either in blind darkness or in the light of Christ. We are born into the first group and can never escape it by virtue of our intelligence or goodness. The Spirit of God alone removes the blindness of the fall from our hearts, enabling us to surrender to our sovereign Redeemer in faith and love.

In his book, *Far as the Curse Is Found*, Michael D. Williams speaks of an atheist who, on considering evidence for the bodily resurrection of Jesus, accepted the truthfulness of the event. When asked how he could remain an atheist yet agree to the authenticity of the resurrection, he answered, "Strange things happen in history."[4] Sister, a blind sinner cannot submit to the lordship of Jesus Christ without the witness of God's Spirit. If our knees are bowing in faith today, then know that God "has delivered us from the domain of darkness and transferred us to the kingdom of his beloved Son, in whom we have redemption, the forgiveness of sins" (Colossians 1:13–14).

Absent of God's Spirit, an unbelieving heart—like Pharaoh's—remains dark and hardened. A heart transformed from darkness to the kingdom of Christ is *enabled* to shine with faith, love, good works, endurance, patience, joy, and gratitude (Colossians 1:3–12). Friend, your Spirit-enabled life of faith shines in a world of deep darkness—so let your light shine before those around you!

The Egyptians dwell in pitch darkness for three days, but the Israelites are surrounded by light. How does the distinction picture all of humanity?

The Spirit of God removes the blindness of the fall from our hearts, enabling faith. How can this truth inspire humility and gratitude for God today?

Pray below for an unbelieving loved one today. Ask God to enable that person to surrender to our sovereign Redeemer in faith and love.

BELIEVE

He has delivered us from the domain of darkness and transferred us to the kingdom of his beloved Son, in whom we have redemption, the forgiveness of sins.

COLOSSIANS 1:13-14

IDENTIFY

It's easy to look at our past with regret and our future with fear. But Christians are given a better perspective. We look back at Christ's finished work and forward to his promised return in view of the gospel. How do both perspectives help you today?

The seahorse is an incredible animal. It's technically a fish, and yet it resembles a Frankenstein combination of creatures. The seahorse has the head of a horse, the tail of a monkey, the nose of an anteater, the skin of a crocodile, the pouch of a kangaroo, and the eyes of a chameleon.[5] I could add to this list, but I'll end with a description of the eyes. The two eyes of the seahorse move independently of each other. This means that the seahorse can see forward *and* backward at the same time. The unique vision of this tiny fish makes it one of the most effective predators of the sea—with a successful hunting rate of over 90 percent.[6] God has equipped this remarkable creature for endurance, and its ability to simultaneously look forward and backward testifies to that. God offers the same eyesight to his people. We see this in Exodus 12:1-20.

Exodus 12:1-20 is structured like a sandwich—there are commandments at the top and bottom and a declaration in the middle. Israel is instructed at the top, Exodus 12:1-11, to look forward in preparation of God's coming salvation. Every Israelite household was to kill an unblemished lamb on the fourteenth day of the month. The animal would be roasted and eaten in haste with unleavened bread. Its blood would be smeared on the doorposts and lintels of Israelite homes. The people's obedience to these detailed commands would demonstrate their trust in God's promised redemption. God was coming to save them through a final plague, so they were to prepare and look forward in anticipation.

God declares his tenth plague in Exodus 12:12-13 (the middle portion of our sandwich structure). He would pass over Egypt by night to strike every firstborn son of the land. Israelites would be spared from this terrible judgment—lambs would die in place of their firstborns. A

All regrets from
your past are
covered in the
shed blood of the
risen Christ.

despairing Pharaoh would drive the Israelites from his land. God would redeem his people. Their salvation would be his work alone—and yet Israel was given a part.

Israel is initially called to look forward in anticipation of God's coming salvation. In Exodus 12:14-20, she's called to look back and remember God's finished work. The fourteenth day of the first month would be memorialized as the Feast of Unleavened Bread or the Passover. Generations of Israelites would pause to remember the day God redeemed his people from Egypt. Exodus 12:1-20 tells us that Israel's salvation belonged to God alone. However, trust in God's promised salvation and remembrance of his faithfulness belonged to his people. This truth stands for Christ's church today.

Yet, if you're like me, a seahorse perspective means you often look back at your past with regrets, while facing the future with fears. There are lurking moments in your past you wish you could change—and there are uncertainties ahead you wish you could control. Sister, if that's you, then consider some familiar words. Jesus looked ahead *and* he encouraged us to look back as he instituted the Lord's Supper. He said this:

> "For I tell you that from now on I will not drink of the fruit of the vine until the kingdom of God comes." And he took bread, and when he had given thanks, he broke it and gave it to them, saying, "This is my body, which is given for you. Do this in remembrance of me.... This cup that is poured out for you is the new covenant in my blood" (Luke 22:18-20).

The Israelites were spared from God's judgment because of the blood of the unblemished lamb. This sign for Israel is fulfilled in Christ, the Lamb of God whose blood is poured out for the forgiveness of sin. Sister, the work for your salvation belongs to Christ alone. Your part today is this: First, fix your eyes ahead to the sure promise of Christ's return and restoration! Second, look back and remember that complete redemption is *already* secured for you. All regrets from your past are covered in the shed blood of the risen Christ.

Friend, exchange your fears and regrets for certain hope as your remember the Lamb who died for you. And anticipate his return.

CONSIDER

▶ How does the structure of Exodus 12:1–20 show us both commandments and a declaration? What does God say he alone will do? What is Israel's part?

....
....
....

▶ How does the Exodus 12 Passover lamb foreshadow the saving work of Christ?

....
....
....

▶ Christians are called to look backward (remembering Christ's finished work) and forward (anticipating his return). How does the life, worship, and communion of the local church help us to sharpen our forward and backward view of the gospel?

....
....
....

BELIEVE

"For I tell you that from now on I will not drink of the fruit of the vine until the kingdom of God comes." And he took bread, and when he had given thanks, he broke it and gave it to them, saying, "This is my body, which is given for you. Do this in remembrance of me." And likewise the cup after they had eaten, saying, "This cup that is poured out for you is the new covenant in my blood."

LUKE 22:18-20

READ

Exodus 14

IDENTIFY

Everyone must tread the waters of death in the end. How does the gospel feed our hope in life *and* battle our fears of death?

The Pilgrim's Progress, written by John Bunyan, is a classic in English literature, remaining in print since its 1678 publication. It tells the allegorical tale of Christian, Bunyan's main character, and his journey from the City of Destruction (this world) to the Celestial City (heaven). Perhaps the story withstands the test of time for its ability to speak to struggling yet persevering Christians of any period. Today, one scene from *The Pilgrim's Progress* begs our attention— Christian's trek through the River of Death.

Bunyan's character faces many obstacles in his journey to the Celestial City. The River of Death, a body of water symbolizing physical death, is the final hurdle. Christian and his companion must wade these waters to reach home. Christian is told that this river will either be deep or shallow, depending on the traveler's faith in the King of the Celestial City.[7] So, according to Bunyan, death is like a river through which all must pass. Some will sink in the waves. Others, trusting in Another, will stand firm. Surely

Bunyan must have had Exodus 14 in mind as he wrote about the River of Death, because the Israelites also passed by faith through the river that brought death to their pursuers.

Israel is liberated by the time we reach Exodus 14. Yahweh kept his promise of redemption. He freed his people from Pharaoh's bondage and guided them to the Red Sea. The king of Egypt should have surrendered to the strong arm of the Lord. Instead, Pharaoh regretted Israel's release and assembled six hundred chariots to pursue them. God would triumph over Pharaoh once more. He works gloriously for the salvation of his people as the Egyptian army is swallowed by the River of Death.

The God of Israel is the hero of Exodus 14. Moses stretched his arms over the sea, but the work was God's. It was the Lord who pushed back the waters throughout the night. It was he who parted the Red Sea, making a dry path for Israel to cross. And it was God who threw the pursuing Egyptian army into confusion. Pharaoh's chariots became useless as the waves fell back into place. In the end, two categories of people stepped into the Red Sea. The first, sheltered by God, found solid footing. The second group, hardened by unbelief, did what all dense things do in water—they sank.

John Bunyan was wise to equate death with water because the Bible does the same. Christian baptism in water is a sign of death and rebirth. The apostle Paul interprets Israel's walk through the Red Sea as their baptism into Moses (1 Corinthians 10:2). Christian baptism symbolizes our death with Christ and our resurrection to newness of life (Romans 6:4). Following Bunyan's allegory, Christians cross the River of Death to enter eternal life. We die to live forever. The unbeliever dies only to die again. We can see a picture of all humanity at the Red Sea.

Dear Sister, everyone must tread the waters of death in the end. Some will sink. Others, united with Christ, will find that Another has gone before them to grant life. That life doesn't begin in heaven—it's at work within you now! So anchor your faith to Christ during today's waves and storms. May he be your steadfast hope in life and in death.

CONSIDER

▶ The apostle Paul interprets Israel's walk through the Red Sea as their baptism. Read Romans 6:1–4. How is Christian baptism a sign of death into new life?

▶ Are you or someone you know afraid of death? How does the reality of union with Christ—you died with him and have been raised with him—speak to that fear?

▶ How is the gospel good news in death? Pray for wisdom to encourage someone who might fear death with the good news of the gospel.

BELIEVE

Do you not know that all of us who have been baptized into Christ Jesus were baptized into his death? We were buried therefore with him by baptism into death, in order that, just as Christ was raised from the dead by the glory of the Father, we too might walk in newness of life.

ROMANS 6:3-4

READ
Exodus 15

IDENTIFY

Have you ever felt your heart changed as you worshipped? During good times and hard times, remembering God's character and works encourages us to sing. And as we worship, we are strengthened and transformed.

Pastor and songwriter Tesfaye Gabbiso experienced some difficult years in Ethiopia. The Ethiopian Empire, led by Emperor Haile Selassie, fell suddenly after centuries of dynastic rule. A military junta overthrew Selassie on September 12, 1974, and established a Marxist communist state.[8] This new government despised religious groups but were especially cruel to Christians. Churches retreated underground as the junta imprisoned, tortured, and killed Christian leaders.[9] It was at this period that Tesfaye Gabbiso became legendary for helping the Ethiopian church sing.

Home churches gathered for secret worship across Ethiopia. Many of these groups lifted their voices in songs composed by Tesfaye Gabbiso. The hymns were written in the local dialect, informed by the experience of persecution, and shaped by Scripture. Just consider these paraphrased lyrics from one of Gabbiso's songs:[10]

I will not deny my Jesus, and worship an object.

I refuse. I refrain.

I will not worship the image/nor kneel down before a man-made thing,

From the burning anger of a Nebuchadnezzar.

My Lord, whom I serve, will surely deliver me.

Gabbiso's lyrics affirmed God's goodness and might. They also engaged the emotions of the singer with Scripture.

Ethiopia's junta government recognized the power of Gabbiso's music and arrested him. Yet, even from his prison cell, he wrote songs for the church to sing.

Sister, many religions chant, but God's people sing! We sing to lament, we sing to rejoice, and we sing to remember the faithfulness of the God who saves. We hear Israel singing to God in our passage today.

Israel stood on the seashore. The people gazed across the Red Sea at the scattered bodies of drowned Egyptians. The nation had witnessed God's glorious power in their salvation *and* in his judgment against their ruthless oppressors. Moses and the people of Israel lifted their voices to sing.

Their song is structured like a sandwich. The top stanzas, Exodus 15:1–10, recall God's glorious triumph over Egypt. The mighty army that pursued to destroy Israel was consumed like stubble in God's righteous judgment. The bottom part of the song, Exodus 15:13–18, looks ahead to the defeat of enemies to come. Canaanite nations would tremble in fear as God planted Israel in his promised land. The meat of the song is found in Exodus 15:11–12. These verses ask a rhetorical question: "Who is like you, O Lord, among the gods?" The theme of Israel's song is clear: whether you look backward or forward, there is no god who compares to the Lord.

Likely, you will raise your voice with brothers and sisters in your local church this coming Sunday. Our corporate worship in song can feel routine at times, while at other times hard circumstances can make worship feel like a chore. Still, Christians are called to sing. The church is exhorted to sing in Ephesians 5:19-20 and Colossians 3:16. Interestingly, both passages connect our singing to gratitude. Worship can transform our worries and doubts to thankfulness as we remember the unsurpassed might and goodness of our God. And like Ethiopian church members facing hard days, our discouragement can turn to gratitude and hope as we remember our God in song.

Whether we face hard persecutions or stunning victories, Christians sing songs that look back at God's power and anticipate his future salvation. Sister, God has revealed himself to be a Savior like none other. So trade worrying for thanksgiving, consider God's character and works (especially those done in your own life)—and sing!

CONSIDER

▶ The Song of Moses and Israel doesn't just boast of God's works in the past. It also looks forward to his power in the coming conquest. How does God's faithfulness in the past encourage our confident hope for the future?

....

....

....

....

▶ The New Testament encourages congregational singing. How does worship in song build unity with others in your local church?

....

....

....

....

▶ Our Sunday morning songs of praise can sometimes feel routine or difficult. Pray below for God to help you remember his unparalleled goodness as you sing this coming Lord's Day!

....

....

....

....

BELIEVE

Let the word of Christ dwell in you richly, teaching and admonishing one another in all wisdom, singing psalms and hymns and spiritual songs, with thankfulness in your hearts to God.

COLOSSIANS 3:16

Take & Share

This week has been all about how God redeems his people. Like the Israelites, we are saved from slavery and death. In Christ, we are free. In Christ we have life forever. We will not be swept away by the river of death. We worship with thankful hearts. Who can you share this good news with this week?

God Provides

This week's readings reveal God as a good Father. He redeems his children from bondage to make himself known to them. Our Father meets all our needs in Christ. Jesus is the Living Water who satisfies eternally, the Bread of Life who sustains us on our journey home, and our true Sabbath rest. He defends his church as we grow together in unity and love. Dear Sister, our Father is generous, so come—drink, eat, and rest.

EXODUS 15:22-18

READ

Exodus 15

IDENTIFY

Seasons of deferred hopes and delayed dreams are often difficult. Are you experiencing that today? Exodus points us to God as our ultimate source of life and satisfaction.

The BBC reported the story of Chaz Powell's near-death experience a few years ago.[1] Powell set out to walk the length of the Zambezi River, the fourth longest river in Africa. He began his solo expedition in Zambia (where the river begins) and trekked across several southeastern African countries. Powell traveled in August to avoid the rainy season. Unfortunately, this decision traded a soggy trip for a blazing one. Temperatures reached 122°F during the day. Powell knew his adventure would bring difficulties, but he never imagined dehydration among them. After all, he was following a *river*; he assumed there would be plenty to drink along the way. Powell packed a limited amount of water.

Powell's path along the Zambezi River took an unfortunate turn near Zimbabwe. The landscape transformed into sharp gorges that rose thousands of feet above the river. Powell could see and hear the currents of the Zambezi, but he couldn't reach the river to drink. He walked ten hours without water on scorching cliffs. His thirst grew, his body temperature soared, he moved sluggishly, and his heart raced. Powell knew he was in danger.

Chaz Powell was experiencing the initial stages of dehydration. Without water, his kidneys would begin to lose function. Without kidneys to filter his blood, cellular waste would build up to cause organ failure and a slow death. Powell gazed at the surging river below him and decided to slide thousands of feet down the gorge to reach the water. He landed with bloody injuries and sat to drink for a full hour before gaining strength.

Sister, we can take water for granted when it's readily available to us, but when it's harder to get, we remember how essential this drink is for life. The same can be true with God. Our seasons of disappointment and dissatisfaction highlight what has always been true—that God is our ultimate source of life and satisfaction. God helps Israel to see this in Exodus 15:22–27.

Three days after singing by the Red Sea, Israel journeyed deep into the wilderness of Shur and ran out of water (Exodus 15:1–22). Their throats grew dry. Their children began to whine for relief. Their parched animals slacked in pace. Israel pressed on until she reached Marah. She looked up and saw a body of water. Perhaps fresh praises rose from dry lips as families rushed to the shoreline. But their hopes were dashed. The waters of Marah were bitter and undrinkable. This disappointment made the Israelites bitter too. They changed their earlier singing to grumbling. God heard them and responded.

The experience of Marah was meant to test the Israelites, not kill them from dehydration. The Israelites had praised the God who controls the waters. Would they trust this same God to nourish them when they were thirsty? Would they cry out to him for help—casting their lament and disappointments at his feet? Would they see *him* as the source of their health and life (Exodus 15:2–26)?

Marah would be the first of Israel's grumbles against God, but Yahweh's mercy is greater than Israel's sins. The Lord sweetened the waters of Marah to refresh his people. Then he provided even more, leading them to Elim, an oasis in the wilderness, a place with twelve springs of water.

We could criticize bitter Israel if not for our own grumblings after praise. Deferred hopes can leave us feeling dry and disappointed with life. We might wonder, "Since the God of my praise is able to satisfy all my prolonged hopes, why doesn't he?"

Sister, seasons of dissatisfaction can be gifts if they guide us to this truth: God himself is our source of life and eternal satisfaction. In Christ, we have water better then Elim's oasis. Like a thirsty person who is desperate for water, tell Jesus all about your disappointments and confess your bitter temptations. When you turn to Jesus, you will always receive sweet mercy. He is the Living Water who will satisfy you with himself (John 4:13–14).

CONSIDER

▶ What unmet needs/desires in your life tempt you to turn from praises to protests?

....

....

....

....

▶ Jesus meets a disappointed and thirsty woman in John. Read John 4:1–45. What does he say to her about himself?

....

....

....

....

▶ How have you encountered Christ during a season of disappointment? Pray to ever know him as the Living Water who can satisfy you with himself!

....

....

....

....

BELIEVE

Jesus said to her, "Everyone who drinks of this water will be thirsty again, but whoever drinks of the water that I will give him will never be thirsty again. The water that I will give him will become in him a spring of water welling up to eternal life."

JOHN 4:13-14

Exodus 16

IDENTIFY

Israel's physical hunger distorts her memories of Egypt from a place of pain to a place of plenty. Do your present difficulties sometimes give you a rosy view of the past and a desire to go back to a destructive way of living?

Dr. Elizabeth Loftus has interesting conversations with strangers on airplanes and at parties. She's a professor of psychology studying memory at the University of California, Irvine. People who learn of her job often share their accounts of short-term memory loss or mention a relative with Alzheimer's disease. Loftus listens and then clarifies with these words: "I don't study when people forget. I study the opposite, when they remember things that didn't happen or remember things that were different from the way they really were. I study false memories."[2]

We tend to think of our memories as "hard drive" faithful recollections of our lived experiences. But research like Loftus's has shown that our memories often shift with our current beliefs, motivations, and even suggestions from others. We remember events differently with time and change. So our memories are more like working documents than fixed hard drives. Dr. Elizabeth Loftus might be interested to know that the Bible reflects some of her research findings on false memory. Our passage today is just such a case.

It was the fifteenth day of the second month since Israel left the land of Egypt. The people were in the wilderness of Sin, between the springs of Elim and Mount Sinai. God had satisfied their thirst for water, but what about their need for food? As they walked miles across wilderness terrain, the Israelites grew hungry and began to reflect on the past. But they skipped over God's provision at Elim to consider their days in Egypt. Their recollections didn't match what actually happened.

The Israelites didn't recount the genocide of their sons or Pharaoh's ruthless demand for hard labor. Instead, they saw themselves banqueting in Egypt and grumbled against their Redeemer: "Would that we had died by the hand of the Lord in the land of Egypt, when we sat by the meat pots and ate bread to the full, for you have brought us out into this wilderness to kill this whole assembly with hunger" (Exodus 16:3). The people God had gathered to himself wished for death because they were hungry.

Israel's disillusionment is shocking—but not as shocking as God's patience. The Lord moved to feed his people bread and meat. The bread came with instructions meant to test Israel's heart. God rained manna, flakes of bread, from heaven. Israel could eat her fill without saving a morsel overnight. God wanted his people to depend on *him* for their daily bread. Some of the Israelites listened. Others disobeyed and found maggot-infested leftover manna in the morning (Exodus 16:20). Their desire to be filled was greater than their trust of God. Have you been there?

Dear friend, blessed are the hungry who look to God. He reveals himself as the faithful provider of daily bread *and* the one whose truth can defeat our false memories of gaining satisfaction from sin. God sent bread from heaven to feed Israel. In Christ, you have the Bread who came down from heaven to give us lasting life (John 6:33–35). His body was broken for those who hunger after past sins, while his grace sustains us on our journeys home. Sister, recall what God has done for you in Christ and let every grumble give way to trust!

▶ Skim Exodus 1, 2, and 5. How is Israel's memory of Egypt contrary to their actual experience?

....

....

....

....

▶ What does God feed Israel in this passage? What instructions come with eating manna? How will this test Israel's trust?

....

....

....

....

▶ Are you tempted to trust sources other than God for your provision? Pray for help to remember God's faithfulness and for grace to grow in your trust of him.

....

....

....

....

BELIEVE

"For the bread of God is he who comes down from heaven and gives life to the world." They said to him, "Sir, give us this bread always." Jesus said to them, "I am the bread of life; whoever comes to me shall not hunger, and whoever believes in me shall never thirst."

JOHN 6:33-35

READ

Exodus 16

IDENTIFY

Sometimes, our hyper-busy schedules testify to self-dependency over trust in the One who came to lighten our burdens. How is Jesus calling you to come and rest in him?

I'll never forget my first experience of stress-induced vertigo. I've felt dizzy before, but *that* dizziness was unmatched. Vertigo is a type of dizziness that makes you feel like your whole world is spinning. The sensation is caused by a disturbance in the vestibular system, which controls our sense of balance from the inner ear. In the case of stress-induced vertigo, elevated levels of stress hormones distort neural communication between the vestibular system and the brain—triggering dizziness and other symptoms.[3] This technical definition became my living reality one weekend as I was hit by a perfect storm of stress.

I was invited to train as an instructor for a beloved Bible teaching ministry. The invitation came with two assignments that required much work. Balancing my usual family obligations with this preparation, plus a few unexpected requests to host friends in our home, brought every ball I was juggling down on my head. I experienced vertigo the night before the training. My bedroom began to spin around. I grew nauseous and knew vomiting might be next. I stumbled clumsily to my bathroom. I felt lightheaded and close to fainting. These terrible symptoms lasted for about an hour—long enough to teach me the lesson that people are made of dust and are called to both work *and* rest. In our passage today, God offers Israel rest. He offers you rest as well.

Our Lord calls
the weary to come
to him for rest.
Jesus is not a
taskmaster but
a gentle and lowly
Redeemer.

It had been less than two months since Israel was liberated from Egypt. Their days of freedom had been few. Still, it seems that this was long enough to dull some memories. Yesterday we read of the Israelites' surprising claim of feasting in Egypt. Had they truly forgotten the sweat and grind of their restless labors? Had thoughts of the Pharaoh who demanded bricks without giving them straw been erased? (Exodus 5:6–9.) What about the whips of the taskmasters who beat Israelites for falling short of the daily quota (Exodus 5:10–14)? Egypt had been a place of toil and difficult work. Yahweh saw the affliction of his suffering people and heard the groans. He came to grant rest.

God isn't a slave master. He's a faithful Father who provides his children with daily bread—and weekly rest. The Lord fed Israel in the desert with a care that Pharaoh would never provide. The Lord instructed his redeemed people to gather a double portion of manna on the sixth day of the week. They would eat the first portion and save the remaining bread for the seventh day. Amazingly, this preserved Sabbath meal lasted without maggots or rot. Israel was free to remain in place on the Sabbath, eating and resting.

However, not every Israelite was quick to observe God's Sabbath ordinance. Some people went out on the seventh day to search for manna. They traded their rest for useless work—revealing their distrust of God. Friend, rest can be equally difficult in our hyper-busy culture. Remaining still, even for a day, can feel impossible. After all, we have dizzying schedules packed with people, good work, and deadlines. While this may be true, Sabbath rest for the Christian isn't a legalistic checklist of dos and don'ts, but instead is a restful trust in the One who upholds all things.

Our Lord calls the weary to come to him for rest—rest from working to save ourselves, rest from the burden of our sins, and rest in his care so we don't think we have to accomplish all our tasks on our own. Jesus is not a taskmaster but a gentle and lowly Redeemer. He carried the yoke we couldn't by fulfilling the demands of God's law, and he lightens our burdens today through the enabling power of his Spirit (Matthew 11:27–30). Dear Sister, let's work *and* rest—trusting the sustainer who holds all things—including us—in his hands.

CONSIDER

▶ How does God's call to Sabbath rest contrast with Pharaoh's treatment of enslaved Israel?

▶ When are you most tempted to depend on yourself for results? How does the gospel—the life, death, resurrection, and indwelling Spirit of Christ—challenge your tendency to work without rest?

▶ Read Matthew 11:27–30. Who holds all things in his hands? Do you find comfort in Jesus's offer of rest? What are some practical ways Jesus is calling you to rest trustfully in him?

BELIEVE

"Come to me, all who labor and are heavy laden, and I will give you rest. Take my yoke upon you, and learn from me, for I am gentle and lowly in heart, and you will find rest for your souls. For my yoke is easy, and my burden is light."

MATTHEW 11:28-30

READ
Exodus 17

IDENTIFY

Every Christian wrestles against darkness and spiritual forces of evil. Moses and Joshua give us a picture of how God provides the power to defeat evil in ourselves and in our world. When you are fighting against evil, what is your hope?

The *Smithsonian* magazine tells the story of the origin of the "Star-Spangled Banner" lyrics.[4] Here's my attempt at summarizing the story: Francis Scott Key, a thirty-five-year-old American lawyer, boarded a British ship during the War of 1812 to negotiate the release of a captured friend. Key succeeded and returned with his companion to his own vessel. Unfortunately, the British detained him there overnight. Key had overheard their plans to attack Baltimore, Maryland, and he was forced to remain on water. Key sat under guard eight miles away from Baltimore Harbor on September 13, 1814, where he would witness the bombardment of Fort McHenry from his boat.

The British were relentless in their attack. They rained shells and rockets on Fort McHenry for twenty-five long hours. Key watched the Battle of Baltimore, certain of a British victory. But as night turned into dawn on September 14, it wasn't the British Union Jack that waved above the fort—it was the American flag. Fort McHenry stood unconquered.

Key's retelling of this night would immortalize the American flag in the national anthem—"The Star-Spangled Banner"—as a symbol of American resolve. Likewise, Exodus 17:8–16 tells its own story of soldiers fighting under a prevailing banner. However, in Exodus, the "banner" isn't just a symbol—it is the source of victory.

In chapter 17, Israel moves from the wilderness of Sin to camp at Rephidim. This will be her last stop before an extended stay at Mount Sinai. The Amalekites—a nomadic tribe descending from Esau—attacked Israel at Rephidim.[5] Until now, Yahweh himself had single-handedly defeated Israel's deadly enemies. The newly freed nation had yet to raise a sword in its own defense. The Amalekites were advancing to strike at Rephidim. How could Israel stand against this desert-hardened tribe?

Moses called Joshua to relay a simple strategy: "Choose for us men, and go out and fight with Amalek. Tomorrow I will stand on the top of the hill with the staff of God in my hand" (Exodus 17:9). Joshua and his men fought as Moses raised the staff of God. Israel prevailed under the lifted staff, but Amalek would triumph whenever a weary Moses dropped his hands. Seeing this, Aaron and Hur sat Moses on a stone and remained to steady his arms on either side. Israel won. The God who gave them water and bread also saved them from enemies—whether they held the sword or not.

Moses built an altar and called its name "The Lord Is My Banner." The word *banner* may bring images of cloth, but the Hebrew word here suggests a "staff."[6] The staff of God—the same one used to turn the waters of the Nile into blood and part the Red Sea—was Israel's flag in battle. Yet the power wasn't in the staff but in the God who worked through the staff. Joshua and his men lifted their eyes to Israel's true Banner—and they prevailed.

Dear Sister, you and I will face enemies fiercer than the Amalekites on our pilgrimage home. Ephesians 6:12 tells us, "For we do not wrestle against flesh and blood, but against the rulers, against the authorities, against the cosmic powers over this present darkness, against the spiritual forces of evil in the heavenly places." The devil's schemes and attacks can distort our desires, our thoughts, and our behaviors. Scripture calls us to stand strong in the strength of Christ, our Banner.

Jesus single-handedly defeated Satan through his death and resurrection. The battle against darkness was won when our Savior was lifted high. So put on Christ's armor, take up the sword of the Spirit, pray always, look to the lifted cross which no enemy can overcome, and stand firm.

CONSIDER

▶ This fight with the Amalekites is Israel's first recorded battle in Exodus. How does God prove to be Israel's source of victory?

....

....

....

....

▶ The lifted and risen Christ is our Banner in every spiritual battle. In what practical ways can you keep your eyes on Christ when wrestling with darkness (see Ephesians 6:10–13)?

....

....

....

....

▶ Aaron and Hur helped to steady Moses's arms in this fight. How might a Christian uplift another believer who is walking through darkness? Is there a specific person whose arms you could steady today?

....

....

....

....

BELIEVE

For we do not wrestle against flesh and blood, but against the rulers, against the authorities, against the cosmic powers over this present darkness, against the spiritual forces of evil in the heavenly places. Therefore take up the whole armor of God, that you may be able to withstand in the evil day, and having done all, to stand firm.

EPHESIANS 6:12-13

READ

Exodus 18

IDENTIFY

Loneliness is a growing reality in our world. Perhaps you are struggling with this today or you know someone who is. What help does God provide for lonely people?

Deepa Sukumar tells a dramatic conversion story.[7] She was born in South India to a culturally Hindu family who defined success by education. Deepa believed that she could earn self-worth through performance. She pursued a career in medicine and matriculated through medical school. Deepa appeared to have a prosperous future ahead of her, and she should have had many hopeful expectations. Instead, she was overwhelmed by feelings of anxiety. If her value was based on her efforts, then who would love her when she fell short? One night, depressed and suicidal, Deepa called out to heaven for help. "Heaven" answered in an interesting way.

Deepa Sukumar's desperate prayer didn't bring a voice from the sky. Rather, God sent a friend. Deepa saw Rohini the next morning. Rohini was a fellow student and a Christian convert from Hinduism. She recognized the despair in Deepa's face and wanted to help. Rohini set aside her schedule to read the Bible to Deepa that morning. She began from the book of Hebrews and read these words: "For he has said, 'I will never leave you nor forsake you'" (Hebrews 13:5). Deepa was suddenly struck by this truth: Jesus's love is steadfast, unconditional, and unearned. Her path toward Christ began that morning as the burden of suicidal grief disappeared. Deepa Sukumar was strengthened by God's Word, which was carried by a friend. The same might be said of Moses in today's passage.

The Israelites journeyed from Rephidim toward Mount Sinai, also known as Horeb. They were nearing the very mountain where Yahweh had first commissioned Moses (Exodus 3:1). Moses had been tending the flock of his father-in-law, Jethro, the priest of Midian, on Mount Horeb when God called him to shepherd Israel. Now news of God's glorious acts had reached Jethro. The priest journeyed to visit Israel in the wilderness and reunite Moses with his wife and two sons. Jethro would bring another valuable gift with him—wise counsel.

Jethro began his visit with worship to Yahweh and then turned his attention to Moses. He watched Israel's shepherd functioning more like a one-man referee. Moses sat alone to settle disputes among the people from morning till evening. Jethro saw the crushing error of the arrangement and spoke up. He advised Moses to be a true mediator—the go-between who represented Israel before God and taught God's law to Israel. Moses could judge difficult cases, but he needed to appoint trustworthy men as magistrates of thousands, hundreds, fifties, and tens. Moses listened to his faither-in-law's voice. The God who had always met directly with Moses now used Jethro's wisdom to guide his prophet. In short, God didn't speak from the sky this time—he sent a friend.

Dear Sister, God doesn't redeem his people in Christ to abandon them. We are united with Christ, his Spirit indwells us, and often, the encouragement of other believers testifies to God's abiding presence with us. We are called to gather with a community of local believers, and the Lord uses the voices of his people (particularly our church elders) to guide us in his Word. The church is to put away falsehood and speak the truth to one another (Ephesians 4:25). We grow in comfort and maturity as we encourage and challenge one another in love. Hearing from heaven might mean hearing the biblical counsel of the brother or sister next to you!

CONSIDER

▶ How did Moses govern Israel's disputes prior to Jethro's advice? How does his system show a blind spot in this godly prophet?

....

....

....

▶ The church's unity in Christ is seen in the care and godly counsel we give to one another (Ephesians 4:25). How have you benefited from the wisdom of your local church?

....

....

....

▶ Do you struggle to give or receive a hard truth from others? Pray for the humility and wisdom to speak truth in love to fellow believers. Ask God to help you see your own blind spots through the biblical counsel of wise friends.

....

....

....

BELIEVE

Therefore, having put away falsehood, let each one of you speak the truth with his neighbor, for we are members one of another.

EPHESIANS 4:25

Take & Share

Consider what you have read and prayed about this week: God provides living water, bread from heaven, rest for our souls, victory over our enemies, and friends to help us on our way in this dark, wearisome world. Who can you share even one of these truths with today?

God Covenants

This week we learn that God redeems his people not only for freedom, but for adoption. He doesn't adopt those who are strong or smart enough to free themselves. We don't obey God to become his children. Rather, he makes children of those he saves. He welcomes us to his table to be his people and to know him as our Father.

EXODUS 19-24

READ
Exodus 19

IDENTIFY

God redeemed you *for* adoption. You don't have to work to become God's child. He adopts you out of his great love for you. What does this good news say about your heavenly Father?

How should it frame your relationship with him?

I heard Maris Blechner's story some years ago. I wasn't an adoptive mom at the time, but her words stayed with me and would ring in my ears at the adoption of my son. Ms. Blechner is a licensed clinical social worker. She specializes in adoption education and has spent years supporting child welfare agencies. Blechner is also an adoptive mom, and it's her personal experience with adoption that I find most inspiring. I'll always remember her definition for adoption.

Blechner's description of adoption was forged through hard conversations. She has heard and suffered from many insensitive comments like this one: "Maris, it's obvious that you love all three of your children. But didn't you feel differently after your son was born? After all, *he's* your blood."[1]

Blechner began crushing these biting remarks with one strong word: *claim*. According to Maris Blechner, an adoptive parent claims her child the same way a birth parent does. To adopt is to embrace a child not genetically related to you as your own. The word *claim* makes sense to me. My adopted son—who looks nothing like me—is as much mine as the daughters who share my smile and thick head of hair. My boy didn't have to earn a place in my heart—he was simply claimed. God adopts his children in a similar way.

Our passage marks three months to the day since Israel departed from Egypt. The nation will reach Mount Sinai today. This is a big moment for Moses. Months ago, he had stood before a burning brush on that very mountain and heard these words: "I will be with you, and this shall be the sign for you ... when you have brought the people out of Egypt, you shall serve God on this mountain" (Exodus 3:12). Moses was ascending Mount Sinai again. God had fulfilled his promised redemption, but he would do much more.

God had a message for Israel—another pledge that began with a reminder:

> "You yourselves have seen what I did to the Egyptians, and how I bore you on eagles' wings and brought you to myself. Now therefore, if you will indeed obey my voice and keep my covenant, you shall be my treasured possession among all peoples, for all the earth is mine; and you shall be to me a kingdom of priests and a holy nation." (Exodus 19:4–6)

Like an attentive momma eagle, Yahweh had flown Israel away to her freedom. Yet God's people were rescued for something greater than freedom itself. They were redeemed for adoption. God brought Israel to *himself*. The nation didn't earn her place with God—she was simply claimed.

Exodus 19 is the chapter immediately before the Ten Commandments. Friend, God rescued enslaved Israel *before* giving them his law. The Israelites didn't earn their salvation through obedience. God would call his people to be holy, but he redeemed them first. Dear Sister, we don't obey God to *become* his children. Rather, in Christ, our Father deliverers us from our enslavement to sin to become his own: "a chosen race, a royal priesthood, a holy nation, a people for his own possession" (1 Peter 2:9). He claims us first, and then he gives us his household rules, along with his Spirit, to enable our obedience.

Adopted children don't always look like their parents. But God adopted us to conform us into his image. In Christ, you can resemble the Father who has eternally claimed you as his own!

What reason does God give for Israel's redemption in Exodus 19:3–6? How is the nation delivered for more than freedom itself?

In Christ, sinners who were far off have now become God's people. Do you believe that you didn't *earn* a place with God but were first chosen? How does this good news grow your gratitude and affection for God?

Ask the Spirit to help you look more like the Father who has claimed you as his own. How can you draw nearer to him today?

BELIEVE

But you are a chosen race, a royal priesthood, a holy nation, a people for his own possession, that you may proclaim the excellencies of him who called you out of darkness into his marvelous light. Once you were not a people, but now you are God's people; once you had not received mercy, but now you have received mercy.

1 PETER 2:9-10

READ

Exodus 20:1–11

IDENTIFY

We live in a day of man-made religions and creeds. Yet God's word offers grace to "religion makers." How can the gospel guard your heart from false gods?

My family is developing a growing tradition. We love to play games together at the dinner table on Sundays. Our current favorite is "Would You Rather." In this game, each person selects a card with a question to answer. Recently our youngest daughter drew this question: "Would you rather start your own company or your own religion?" She read the words and was perplexed by the connection between a company and a religion. I must admit that I was equally struck by the association. According to the makers of this game, you can set the terms for your religion like an entrepreneur determining the policies for a company. The question appeared silly until I considered it further.

In truth, man-made religions abound. And tragically, some falsely call their made-up religion Christianity. As I write, there's a video buzzing around the internet that shows a congregation reciting a creative version of the Apostle's Creed—one filled with modern ideologies and contradictions to the Bible.[2] We can bemoan these trends, and yet, even a Christian committed to Scripture can slip into some deceptive beliefs. Perhaps, like me, you've entertained this thought: "It's my good works that bring answered prayers and God's favor. I earn God's pleasure and love through good behavior." We become inventors of a false creed at these moments, replacing the God of the Bible for a judge who rules by *our* standards. Our passage today speaks grace to "religion makers."

God speaks directly to Israel for the first time in their journey. He gives them ten foundational moral commandments. The first four deal with Israel's relationship with him. God had claimed Israel as his own—they were his people by right of redemption. Like a husband's righteous jealousy for his wife's love, Yahweh would have no other gods before him. Israel was told not to make or bow down to a carved image. They were never to take God's name in vain. And they were commanded to keep the Sabbath day holy, reflecting trust in their God who created the world in six days and rested on the seventh. In all, Exodus 20:1-11 shouts a clear truth: God himself sets the terms for his people's worship—and that's a gift.

God delivered Israel from slavery to reveal *himself* to them. The nation didn't have to rely on their creative imagination to worship the Lord; Yahweh spoke to give moral laws that expressed his own holy character and displayed his nature to those he had redeemed for relationship. In short, God didn't speak laws just to restrict, but also to make himself known. And so, as the story of redemption continues, the God who forbade the carving of an image would send down his own image in time.

Jesus Christ, the image of the invisible God, came to reveal the fullness of God to his people (Colossians 1:15, 19-20). Christ, our Redeemer, will have no other gods before him. And that's a gift to us! Jesus is better than any man-made god or ideology we could invent. He sets the terms for our relationship with him, and he does so to bring us near and make the Father known (John 17:25-26). In Christ, we see that we cannot approach God through the inventions of our own imagination or through good works. By his death and resurrection, Jesus Christ, the image of the invisible God, has reconciled us to his Father. Dear Sister, believe this good news and dismiss every competing god and creed. Bow down to the God revealed through Scripture—and none other.

CONSIDER

▶ See Exodus 20:1. Moses has conveyed God's words to Israel up to this point. Who is speaking *directly* to Israel in Exodus 20:1–17? How does the speaker's identity heighten the seriousness of his message?

....
....
....
....

▶ See Exodus 20:2. How does God identify himself to Israel in the giving of the Ten Commandments? How should these words inspire Israel's allegiance and singular devotion to God?

....
....
....
....

▶ How can you guard your heart against false worship? Pray for yourself (and for others) who invent their own religions—especially those who falsely espouse Christianity.

....
....
....
....

BELIEVE

"You shall not make for yourself a carved image, or any likeness of anything that is in heaven above, or that is in the earth beneath, or that is in the water under the earth. You shall not bow down to them or serve them, for I the LORD your God am a jealous God."

EXODUS 20:4-5A

READ

Exodus 20:1–17

IDENTIFY

We cannot love others in our own strength. Thankfully, God's Spirit empowers Christians to love. How does your love for neighbors reflect God's own love for you?

Bible teacher and author Mary Wilson Hannah tells the remarkable story of Reverend Willie Jenkins Jr.[3] Reverend Jenkins lived in Pearl, Mississippi, in the 1960s. He worked to racially integrate the school system in Pearl and was violently targeted as a result. Harassment came from various corners, including a group of white teenagers who would persistently drive through his neighborhood to firebomb homes. The teenagers came one evening to intimidate Jenkins. The minister and his sons stood outside their property, ready to protect their family as needed. The young men drove to the house intending violence, but they were met by the unexpected. They ran out of gas directly in front of Jenkins's house.

The Reverend Jenkins stood facing the teens that had come to damage his home. His sons stood by their father, uncertain of his next move. Reverend Jenkins walked forward and picked up a glass bottle. He broke it on the ground. His sons assumed a defensive attack would follow. However, instead of approaching the teens, Jenkins moved toward his own car. He took the broken bottle and began siphoning gasoline. Everyone at the scene stared as Jenkins bent down to refill the empty tank of his harassers. He finished and stood up with bloody hands from the broken glass. Reverend Willie Jenkins Jr. displayed a neighborly love that goes beyond natural inclination. This is the love prescribed in our passage today.

The Israelites stood at the base of Mount Sinai to listen to the words of their Redeemer. The Lord spoke directly to Israel to give Ten Commandments. The first four, which we just considered, dealt with his relationship with his people. The remaining six were life-giving commands for human-to-human relationships. God told the Israelites to honor their parents. He forbade murder, adultery, theft, and false testimony against a neighbor. Last, God commanded his people against covetousness—setting longing eyes on a neighbor's possession. Altogether, the Ten Commandments embody the heart of the soon-to-come Mosaic Law. We might summarize the ten together in this way: love God with all your heart and love your neighbor as yourself (Matthew 22:34–40). It's a simple summary, but a difficult mandate for sinners.

There's nothing easy about these Ten Commandments. One might think that hearing an audible speech from God would motivate total obedience. Sadly, the Israelites who stood at Sinai that day would soon violate God's orders in a dramatic way (Exodus 32). Fallen humans need more than motivation to follow God's law. Our track records tell an ugly truth: we covet, we lie, we dishonor parents in childhood and in adulthood. We don't love God with all our hearts, and we don't love our neighbors as ourselves. Is there hope for us? There is. The hope is found in a Man whose stunning display of love goes beyond the natural.

Friend, the gospel shouts good news when we first remember the bad news. Human beings need more than motivation to keep God's commandments because we are inherent enemies of God, people made *innately* sinful through the fall of our first parents—Adam and Eve (Genesis 3). But "God so loved the world, that he gave his only Son" (John 3:16; see also Romans 5:10). Jesus came to take our place in two incredible ways: First, he lived for us. The man Jesus satisfied every law of God. He came to love God and neighbor perfectly, and, amazingly, his sinless record is credited to those who trust in him. Second, Christ died for us. Jesus bore the curse that comes from disobeying God's commandments. His sacrificial death for born enemies like you and me is the truest picture of neighbor love.

And there's more. Jesus lives today to *empower* his people to love God and others as we have been loved (John 15:12–13). We have more than self-motivation, so let's stun the world by our Spirit-enabled love!

We don't obey God to become his children. Rather, in Christ, our Father deliverers us from our enslavement to sin to become his own.

CONSIDER

▶ Read Matthew 22:34–40. How do the Ten Commandments capture the heart of the first and second greatest commandments?

....

....

....

▶ Read John 15:12–17. How did Jesus show the truest picture of neighbor love? How did he transform born enemies into friends?

....

....

....

....

▶ Consider how you can tangibly express love to a neighbor. Write some ideas down, beginning with a prayer for that person.

....

....

....

....

BELIEVE

"This is my commandment, that you love one another as I have loved you."

J O H N   1 5 : 1 2

READ

Exodus
20:1–21

IDENTIFY

The people who met God in the Bible were all terrified. After all, fear is the proper response of sinners before a holy God. We need help to approach him. Today we will think about how Moses was a mediator for Israel; he points to Jesus, the mediator given for you and me. Fully God and fully human, Jesus stands in the gap between us and God.

I'll always remember the late R. C. Sproul's description of *Inner Sanctum*.[4] Sproul, who grew up before the advent of television, was a fan of a 1940s horror mystery radio program. Sproul recalled his days as a boy, listening intently to the show's opening lines. He would hear the creaking sounds of a burial vault open as a voice shrieked the words, "Inner Sanctum!" The title meant little to Sproul as a boy. It was later, with some theological training under his belt, that he realized the deeper meaning of the name.

The noun *inner sanctum* can be translated as "inside a sacred place" or "within the holy." Whether intentional or not, the producers of the show *Inner Sanctum* were connecting the idea of holiness to fear. According to Sproul, fallen humanity naturally fears the presence of a holy God. The Bible verifies this truth, and the present passage provides a case in point.

Today, we find a shaken Israel at the foot of Mount Sinai. God had spoken directly to them in giving the Ten Commandments. His words weren't long, but they came with a startling multisensory experience. The nation heard roaring thunder and watched the sky flash with lightning. They saw no trumpeters, and yet the sound of trumpets blared in their ears. Smoke erupted from a shaking Mount Sinai and filled their noses. Israel stood far from God and trembled. When they spoke, it wasn't in praise, but in a desperate plea to Moses.

The nation begged for a mediator: "You speak to us, and we will listen; but do not let God speak to us, lest we die" (Exodus 20:19). Gripped by fear, Israel quivered away from the mountain at a distance. How could they ever abide with their Redeemer? How can sinful people dwell with a holy God?

We often study the Ten Commandments without considering Israel's terrified response at the occasion. If Yahweh gave his moral law to reveal his character and direct Israel's relationship with him and with each other, then the people's determined retreat seems to counter his purposes. But Moses explains with these words of comfort: "Do not fear, for God has come to test you, that the fear of him may be before you, that you may not sin" (Exodus 20:20). It's right for sinners to take God's holiness seriously. In fact, awe-inspiring fear can be a gracious deterrent to sin. Moses reasoned with Israel, then he shouldered the role of a mediator. He drew near to the thick darkness where God was (Exodus 20:21). In Moses, we catch a glimpse of the greater Mediator who approached God to exchange our panic for peace.

Jesus alone—truly God and truly a sinless man—could stand within the inner sanctum of God's presence without fear of judgment. And yet he stood there to bear our judgment. Today Christ invites you to a different mountain by virtue of *his* blood and perfect obedience of God's moral law. Sister, there's no need to tremble at the foot of Mount Sinai. Christ welcomes you to ascend Mount Zion with confident joy (Hebrews 12:18–24). In him, *joy* is the natural response of sinners declared righteous before a holy God. A Mediator better than Moses brings you to the inner sanctum of God's presence to receive mercy and grace. So draw near to him—not in fear but with gratitude, awe-inspired reverence, and a readiness to hear his voice and obey his Word (Hebrews 12:25–29).

What sights, sounds, and smells accompanied God's words to Israel in Exodus 20:1–21? What was Israel's reaction?

Read Hebrews 12:18–29. How does this passage picture Mount Sinai and Mount Zion? How has Christ made you a citizen of the latter?

Do you fear God's eternal judgment despite Christ's work on your behalf? Pray that your gratitude, reverence for God, and close communion with him would reflect your new covenant life on Mount Zion.

BELIEVE

For you have not come to what may be touched, a blazing fire and darkness and gloom and a tempest and the sound of a trumpet and a voice whose words made the hearers beg that no further messages be spoken to them. For they could not endure the order that was given, "If even a beast touches the mountain, it shall be stoned." Indeed, so terrifying was the sight that Moses said, "I tremble with fear." But you have come to Mount Zion and to the city of the living God, the heavenly Jerusalem, and to innumerable angels in festal gathering, and to the assembly of the firstborn who are enrolled in heaven, and to God, the judge of all, and to the spirits of the righteous made perfect, and to Jesus, the mediator of a new covenant, and to the sprinkled blood that speaks a better word than the blood of Abel.

HEBREWS 12:18-24

READ

Exodus 24

IDENTIFY

Who do you welcome to your table?

Is your circle small? Do you only include a select few family and friends, or do you invite all kinds of people to eat with you? Read about the great feast of the Lord, and think about how to live a welcoming life today.

I had a brutal middle-school experience. I remember scenes that could have been from some prime-time adolescent drama. My school had its share of merciless bullies and inflexible social hierarchies. The lunchroom told you everything about your popularity status. You had to be athletic enough, fashionable enough, or just plain cool enough to sit at certain tables. As a recent African immigrant who spoke English as a second language, you might guess that I was on the lower end of the middle-school pecking order. So imagine my shock at being invited to a "cool table" one day. My stay there would not be long.

A good-natured popular girl had asked me to join her for lunch. She was happy for me to sit next to her, but less secure kids around her saw my presence as a demotion to their own ranking. Their table couldn't practice inclusivity and remain remarkable at the same time. They asked me to leave—and I did. The discouragement from that moment has long faded into an interesting memory. And because God can redeem any situation for his good purposes, even this grim childhood event proves useful—it reminds me of the importance of welcoming others. A table that brings far-off people near can point us to the God who does the same. We catch a glimpse of that in our passage today.

Exodus 24 might seem a bit surprising to those who have been reading the book sequentially to this point. Israel had just retreated from God in fear at the giving of the Ten Commandments (Exodus 20:18–21). Now no less than seventy elders are seen scaling Mount Sinai for a visit and a meal with Yahweh. What happened between chapters 20 and 24? Exodus 21–23 can help us.

God didn't withdraw from the nation that stood far off from him, and he didn't stop speaking after giving the Ten Commandments. God gave them a long list (three chapters!) of civil and penal codes to govern Israel's communal and worship life. These moral imperatives would be the terms of God's covenant with Israel. Moses relayed God's words, and the people received them with surprising eagerness. They answered with one voice, "All the words that the Lord has spoken we will do" (Exodus 24:3). With this vow of obedience, God ratified his covenant with Israel. Moses killed an animal and threw half of its blood onto the people (Exodus 24:6–8). God consecrated Israel as his own through the shed blood of a sacrificial animal. He then invited the elders to a meal.

Moses and a group of elders traveled up Mount Sinai to eat and drink with their God. Yahweh welcomed them to his table without the penalty of death (Exodus 24:11). Israel moved from fear to fellowship with God—yet this access to God's presence was exclusive. A privileged few were welcomed, and only for a moment to see the floor of God's throne. We might marvel at the progress between Exodus 20 and 24, while still wondering, is this as good as it gets? The gospel gives an emphatic no to that question.

Friend, our followship with God on Mount Zion will not compare to this one on Mount Sinai. We have been consecrated to God through the shedding of a greater blood that welcomes *all* of God's people to a feast. Our Father is preparing rich food full of marrow and well-aged wine (Isaiah 25:6)! He will gather his children to eat and behold his *face*. Our Christian communion today is a foretaste of that greater feast to come. Sister, set a table that intentionally welcomes the far-off people in your church community. Eat, drink, and point to the host who does the same (Ephesians 2:13).

CONSIDER

▶ See Exodus 24:9-11. Who is invited to come up the mountain to God? What do they do? What do they see? How does God extend grace to them?

....

....

....

....

▶ Read Isaiah 25 with attention to verses 6–8. How does the prophet Isaiah envision Zion, the mountain of the Lord? What kind of banquet will God hold, and where will his guests come from?

....

....

....

....

▶ Is there someone in your own church you could get to know better over a meal? Pray below for the Lord to make your own table a place of welcome for diverse and varied people.

....

....

....

....

BELIEVE

But now in Christ Jesus you who once were far off have been brought near by the blood of Christ.

EPHESIANS 2:13

Take & Share

What one thing did you learn about God this week from your study of Exodus that you could share with a friend? Perhaps you could start with how we are God's treasured possession, and he carries us on eagles' wings and invites us to his table. However, to be God's treasured possession we need a mediator, because he is holy and, apart from him, we are not. Jesus is a better mediator than Moses. Point someone to him this week.

God Reveals

This week the action pauses within the drama of Exodus for God to give his people the plans for his earthly sanctuary. The tabernacle and the priests who minster in it must reflect the glory and beauty of the Redeemer. But God's presence won't remain confined to this physical space. His Son will come as the true temple to establish his church, the new dwelling place of God on earth. In Christ, we are the temple of God today. May our faith, prayers, and service reflect God's glory and beauty!

EXODUS 25-31

READ

Exodus 25–31

IDENTIFY

Are you quicker to see God's demands for your holiness before noticing his ultimate end for his holy people?

The longest speech in Exodus reveals God's desire to dwell with his people. How can this truth encourage you as you draw nearer to God today?

While writing today's devotional, I asked two Bible students this question: What topic does God make the longest speech about in the book of Exodus? They both answered, the Ten Commandments and the Law. God's law and provision for Israel's holiness are certainly central to the story Moses is telling. But what if God's redeeming and sanctifying work aims for another purpose we don't always remember? Today we catch a glimpse of this intention within the longest monologue of Exodus.

It's been said that the mouth speaks what the heart delights in (Luke 6:45). These words prove true in my home! My young son will chat for a long time about Legos. In a similar vein, my quiet cookbook-reading daughter loves nothing better than to discuss novel recipes. Given the right topic, even an introverted person becomes a talker. God takes the microphone today to address Moses. He speaks from Exodus 25–31—seven straight chapters! Friend, God's longest speech reveals his heart for his beloved people. He rescued and set Israel apart to *live* with him!

God speaks to prepare his sanctuary among his redeemed. Yahweh's words carry the authority of a Father who is building a house to dwell with his children (Exodus 29:45-46). He meets with Moses to provide specific instructions for the pattern of the tabernacle and the ministry around it. He gives precise numbers, types of materials, and names of those he wishes to employ to his service. God warns Moses to make everything after the pattern revealed to him (Exodus 25:40). The longest monologue in Exodus ends with these words:

> And [the LORD] gave to Moses, when he had finished speaking with him on Mount Sinai, the two tablets of the testimony, tablets of stone, written with the finger of God. (Exodus 31:18)

Moses is the storyteller, but the plot is God's. And the heart of this narrative shows a Redeemer who comes to reside with his people.

Perhaps, like the Bible students I questioned, you're quicker to see God's demands for your holiness before noticing his ultimate purpose for his holy people. If so, know that God's plan has always been to dwell with you! What we find in the story of the exodus is true for the entire story of Scripture—God intends to live with his people! His long speech in today's passage details his sanctuary among the Israelites, but it gets better as the Bible continues.

In time, God would prepare a much better tabernacle—the body of his own Son (Hebrews 10:5, 10). Jesus took on flesh and came to "pitch his tent" on earth (John 1:14). He came to temporarily abide—but eternally redeem. He offered up his flesh for our redemption. Christians are sanctified through the offering of the body of Jesus Christ so that they can dwell with God through his Spirit today—and see him face-to-face one day. Dear Sister, remember this sweet truth as you draw near to a God who delights to be with you!

CONSIDER

▶ Read Exodus 29:45–46. Why did God give such careful instructions concerning his house? What was his ultimate purpose for the tabernacle and the ministry around it?

....
....
....

▶ Are you quicker to see God's demands for your holiness before noticing his ultimate purpose for his holy people? How does God's desire to dwell with you encourage you to draw closer to him?

....
....
....

▶ The mouth speaks what the heart delights. How do your conversations reflect your delight in God? Pray that his presence would be your ever-growing delight!

....
....
....

BELIEVE

I will dwell among the people of Israel and will be their God. And they shall know that I am the Lord their God, who brought them out of the land of Egypt that I might dwell among them. I am the Lord their God.

EXODUS 29:45-46

READ

Exodus 25

IDENTIFY

Is it hard for you to be generous? We live in a world where we are constantly told we need more—not less! Giving can seem counterintuitive. Our passage today shows us God's generous heart to his people and gives us meaning for our giving.

Don and Carol Richardson were young and newly married when they heard God's call to take the gospel to distant places. The couple bundled up their infant son and moved to New Guinea, an island in Australia. They would live for years among the Sawi people, who were seminomadic cannibals.

God protected the Richardson family. They were received by the Sawi, who were interested in their technology and modern tools. Don and Carol were welcomed among the people, and gospel work seemed promising until Don encountered a difficult roadblock. The tribe heard the story of Jesus's crucifixion and instantly praised *Judas* for his cunning betrayal. Judas, not Jesus, emerged as the hero to these warriors who valued deceit and violence. Don Richardson felt stuck until he observed a fascinating Sawi tradition.[1] The Sawi tribe ended feuds between villages by exchanging two baby boys. One family from each of the respective communities would trade and raise an infant son for the sake of peace. In other words, reconciliation required the precious gift of a son. Don Richardson used the analogy of this ritual to turn the eyes of the Sawi from Judas to the God who gave the gift of his own Son to bring peace to sinners. Today's passage reminds us of that generous Father who calls his people to give generously in turn.

Exodus 25 begins with a charge. God told Moses to take a contribution from the Israelites. This collection would be an offering to God. Notice the repetition of the words "for me" in Exodus 25:2: "Speak to the people of Israel, that they take for me a contribution. From every man whose heart moves him you shall receive the contribution for me." These articles would be used to construct God's tabernacle. Israelite men, representing families, were to give freely to the Lord without compulsion. And interestingly, the items God asked for were the same ones he told them to take from Egypt on their way out of town.

God asked his people to contribute "gold, silver, and bronze, blue and purple and scarlet yarns and fine twined linen, goats' hair, tanned rams' skins, goatskins, acacia wood, oil for the lamps, spices for the anointing oil and for the fragrant incense, onyx stones, and stones for setting" (Exodus 25:3–7). These are opulent treasures for a band of wilderness-wandering, formerly enslaved people to own. But God had been generous to Israel at her freedom. "The Lord had given the people favor in the sight of the Egyptians, so that they let them have what they asked. Thus they plundered the Egyptians" (Exodus 12:36). Now Israel was to give freely to God the gifts God himself had liberally provided. Sister, he asks the same of you and me.

The New Testament encourages Christian generosity without coercion. We have the example of the early church meeting the needs of struggling Christians. Paul tells the church in Corinth that this ministry reaches beyond the saints to produce "many thanksgivings to God" (2 Corinthians 9:11–12). Our generous contributions for the care of others—especially those in the household of faith—bring glory to God. Our willing gifts are small pictures of the One who gave us far more than rich plunder. For our peace, God offered the inexpressible gift of his own Son (2 Corinthians 9:15)! What is too costly for us to give back to him?

CONSIDER

▐ How does the plunder of the Egyptians show both God's favor for Israel and the provision by which he would tabernacle among them?

....

....

....

▐ Generosity can be a difficult area of testing for many of us. How does remembering God's gift of Christ and his daily care for his children encourage cheerful giving?

....

....

....

▐ How does your partnership with your local church help to meet the needs of other saints? Pray that your gospel-empowered generosity might produce thanksgivings to God!

....

....

....

....

BELIEVE

You will be enriched in every way to be generous in every way, which through us will produce thanksgiving to God. For the ministry of this service is not only supplying the needs of the saints but is also overflowing in many thanksgivings to God.

2 CORINTHIANS 9:11-12

READ

Exodus 26

IDENTIFY

God has broken down strong barriers to draw his redeemed to himself. Once barred, today Christ's church has open access to God's throne room! How can you encourage yourself and others with this glorious truth?

I live in the nation's capital and have driven past the Pentagon countless times. Washington, DC, residents are close to many prominent national historic buildings. My backyard is packed with American history and yet—unlike tourists—I don't always explore these landmarks. Last month I played the role of a tourist and finally toured the Pentagon, which taught me the meaning of "restricted access."

The Pentagon is the headquarters of the United States Department of Defense. The building and grounds are highly secured. While thousands of tourists visit its halls each year, their presence is carefully controlled. For instance, I had to arrive sixty minutes before my tour to be scanned and briefed on security guidelines. Personal electronic devices (like cellphones and smartwatches) are not permitted on Pentagon tours, so I had to place my phone in a lockbox until the end. My group was assigned two tour guides, both active military service members. These men monitored us closely, with one positioned in front of the group and the other behind us. It was plain to see that public access to the Pentagon is highly restricted. The same might be said for the tabernacle described in Exodus.

God reveals his architectural pattern for the tabernacle in today's reading, and it calls for many curtains. God told Moses to create two curtain structures. The first would be the tabernacle itself: ten linen curtains of blue, purple, and scarlet, woven skillfully with cherubim designs. These curtains would contain two chambers— the Holy Place and the Most Holy Place (Exodus 26:31- 33). An outer tent, made of eleven goat hair curtains, would be placed around the tabernacle for its protection (Exodus 26:7). The entire structure would represent God's dwelling place among Israel. At the same time, its many curtains signaled God's holiness and inaccessibility. Only the high priest entered the Most Holy Place—and only once a year on the day he atoned for the sins of the people (Leviticus 16). A holy God among a sinful people meant careful barriers for Israel's sake. In other words, God drew near to his people and access to his presence was still restricted. Yet one day God himself would rip apart the curtains.

One dark afternoon, many centuries after the exodus, the curtain that separated the Most Holy Place from the outer courts of the temple in Jerusalem was torn in two from top to bottom (Matthew 27:51). Jesus, our Great High Priest, entered the holy places and made full atonement for our sins through the sacrifice of his blood. The way to God was opened for us through the broken body of Christ (Hebrews 10:11-14, 19-20). Friend, you have access to God's presence. But there's more! God's presence is no longer confined to the inner chambers of Israel's temple; instead, his presence abides with everyone who trusts in Jesus.

Sister, take an intentional look at the members of your local congregation this coming Sunday. Look at Christ's church and rejoice in this truth: access to God's throne room, once restricted to one man once a year, is now available to every brother and sister beside you. Like a high-level Pentagon employee with unrestricted access, God's people are free to approach his throne room with confidence. Remind yourself and others that our Redeemer will break every barrier to draw his church nearer and make himself known.

God's people are free to approach his throne room with confidence.

CONSIDER

▶ How did the curtains of the tabernacle offer Israel some access to God while also guarding her from God's consuming holiness?

....

....

....

....

▶ Read Hebrews 10. How has Christ opened a way for us to God's presence?

....

....

....

....

▶ Do you pray with the confidence of a Christian who is welcomed into God's throne room? Remember the barrier Christ has opened for you, and praise him!

....

....

....

....

BELIEVE

Therefore, brothers, since we have confidence to enter the holy places by the blood of Jesus, by the new and living way that he opened for us through the curtain, that is, through his flesh.

HEBREWS 10:19-20

READ
Exodus 30

IDENTIFY

Scripture tells Christians to pray without ceasing, but we're not always careful to follow that commandment. How is your prayer life?

How does God's welcoming nature help you to pray in all situations?

David Livingstone died the way he lived. The missionary explorer took the gospel to parts of Africa no European had previously seen. Livingstone's footprints touched southern, central, and eastern Africa before his death. He's remembered for documenting geographic features of the continent, for confronting the Dutch and Portuguese for their dehumanizing treatment of Africans, and for his passionate antislavery advocacy.[2] These deeds are note-worthy, but Livingstone's last act before his death points to his source of wisdom and strength.

David Livingstone was discovered dead on May 1, 1873. He was sixty years old and had lived in Africa for half his life. His attendants saw him to bed that evening and woke to find him kneeling by his bedside, as if in prayer.[3] It was soon evident that Livingstone had died in that position. Apparently, the last disease that came to take his life couldn't stop him from praying. The tireless Christian had prayed his way across Africa, and he also prayed on his journey to a heavenly home. Livingstone's example reminds Christians of the need for constant prayer—just as today's passage does.

Moses continues his conference with God on Mount Sinai. Yahweh summoned Israel's mediator to reveal his divine pattern for the tabernacle and its ministry. God gave details for the altar of incense. This altar, made of pure gold, was to be placed directly in front of the curtain that separated the Holy Place from the Most Holy Place. The high priest Aaron and his descendants were to burn morning and evening incense on this altar throughout their generations. The sweet spices for the incense were ordered by God to be formulated by an expert perfumer (Exodus 30:34–38). The fragrant smoke it produced would be holy to the Lord and would rise perpetually before him as a pleasing aroma. Amazingly, this smoke is later associated with the prayers of God's people!

King David remembered the altar of incense when he wrote Psalm 141:2: "Let my prayer be counted as incense before you, and the lifting up of my hands as the evening sacrifice!" David asked that his petitions might ascend like sweet fragrance mounting up to God's throne. Revelation 8:4 echoes David's plea. There we read, "the smoke of the incense, with the prayers of the saints, rose before God." This image of prayer soaring like incense isn't limited to the symbolic language of the Psalms or the book of Revelation. We find it in the Gospels as well.

Luke, the Gospel writer, begins his orderly account of Christ with a striking story. He speaks of a priest named Zechariah, a descendant of Aaron who was "chosen by lot to enter the temple of the Lord and burn incense" (Luke 1:9). There were multitudes praying outside as Zechariah began the ritual. The old priest expected to burn incense and exit from the holy place as his forefathers had done so many times before him. But Luke tells us that an angel met with Zechariah to announce the gift of a son and the coming of the long-expected Savior. Sister, consider how many multitudes of people had prayed for God to send the Savior promised in the garden (Genesis 3:15) from the days of Aaron to Zechariah. Prayers of faith—like sweet smoke—were lifted for centuries to God's throne. The Lord heard each one.

Dear Sister, let your prayers be unceasing, like sweet incense reaching perpetually up to your God (1 Thessalonians 5:17). After all, if the approach of death itself couldn't mute David Livingstone's prayers, then what situation is worthy of your silence? Let your life be marked by ever-ascending prayers to a God who hears them.

CONSIDER

▶ Read Exodus 30:6–8. How many times each day and for how many generations were the Israelites to burn incense on the altar before the Most Holy Place?

_____

_____

_____

▶ How do later passages in the Bible connect the image of incense with persistent prayer (see Psalm 141:2; Luke 1:5–17; Revelation 5:8; 8:3–4)? How does the altar of incense play a role in Luke's account of Christ?

_____

_____

_____

▶ The One who ordered perpetual incense desires to hear your unceasing prayers before his throne. How is your prayer life? How does David Livingstone's example challenge you to pray often?

_____

_____

_____

BELIEVE

Pray without ceasing. Give thanks in all circumstances; for this is the will of God in Christ Jesus for you.

1 THESSALONIANS 5:17-18

READ

Exodus 31:1–11

IDENTIFY

Some God-given gifts will seem more glorious than others. Still, *each* member of Christ's body is called to serve for the sake of the whole. What is your Spirit-empowered gift, and how does it help to build up the church?

The human body is more astounding than we often realize. The structure and function of our bodies compare to nothing else in the universe. The human body is powerful and capable of spectacular feats. Yet some of the biggest jobs the body performs are done with the help of its smallest members.

Just consider the teeny hairs in your inner ear! There are small hair cells inside your inner ear that help you to hear. The hairs convert sound waves into the nerve signals that your brain recognizes as sound.[4] These hairs differ from the kind that grow on your head. First, your inner ear hairs cannot regrow. This means that hearing loss caused by hair cell damage or decline is permanent.[5] In short, the quality of your hearing rests on the health of the tiny hairs in your inner ear. It's stunning how the various parts of our body work together for our well-being. Even the seemingly fragile and unseen members have their role. The same can be said of God's covenant community, which we see in today's passage.

We are introduced to Bezalel and Oholiab in chapter 31. Like two lesser-known members of the human body that suddenly prove vital, Bezalel and Oholiab emerged in the narrative with key roles. God says to Moses, "See, I have called by name Bezalel the son of Uri, son of Hur, of the tribe of Judah, and I have filled him with the Spirit of God, with ability and intelligence, with knowledge and all crafts-manship" (Exodus 31:2–3). The God who gave precise instructions for the construction of his earthly sanctuary selected a building crew by name. God would super-naturally empower Bezalel (along with Oholiab) to erect the tabernacle and altars, its furnishings, utensils, incense, and priestly garments—everything God required to dwell among Israel (Exodus 31:7–11).

Considering his divine election for this job, it is interesting that the name *Bezalel* means "in God's shadow."[6] This gifted designer wouldn't work by the genius of his own creativity but would construct the tabernacle in the shadow of a higher Archi-tect. God sends Bezalel and Oholiab this warning through Moses: "According to all that I have commanded you, they shall do" (Exodus 31:11). These craftsmen had to be careful to follow God's design. They were building a tabernacle to reflect "the true tent that the Lord set up, not man," as Hebrews 8:2 explains. Bezalel would labor in God's shadow *and* the structure he raised would itself be a shadow of a heavenly sanctuary (Hebrews 8:5). God's residence among Israel was only a taste of a future reality. Bezalel's and Oholiab's Spirit-empowered work pointed forward to the day God would fully tabernacle with his church in Christ.

Like a well-performing human body, the church of Christ is one body made up of various members. God gives grace to each believer according to the measure of his gift to build up the body of Christ (Ephesians 4:7–12). Each member of the church is enabled by the Spirit to contribute to the life of the body. Some God-given gifts might seem more glorious than others. Still, *each part* working properly "makes the body grow so that it builds itself up in love" (Ephesians 4:16). The grace given to Bezalel and Oholiab at Sinai was unique. Yet, your Spirit-empowered gift today is given for the benefit of Christ's church! So, Sister, use your gift—whether it be teaching, serving, or evangelism—to build up God's temple on earth! Serve well in the shadow of the One who is preparing his people for a heavenly tent, which will not be made by human hands.

CONSIDER

▶ Considering Hebrews 8:5, why does God warn Bezalel and Oholiab to follow each God-ordained detail?

....

....

....

▶ In what ways do you contribute to the life of your local church? Instead of thinking about your gifts as either "big" or "small," consider how the Lord is using your gifts to build others up in love.

....

....

....

....

▶ God gives grace to each believer according to the measure of his gift (Ephesians 4:7). Pray for God's help to view your gifts (whatever they may be) as a grace from him. Pray below for the help to serve "in God's shadow"—that is, with the strength that he supplies.

....

....

....

....

BELIEVE

Rather, speaking the truth in love, we are to grow up in every way into him who is the head, into Christ, from whom the whole body, joined and held together by every joint with which it is equipped, when each part is working properly, makes the body grow so that it builds itself up in love.

EPHESIANS 4:15-16

Take & Share

This week we meditated on how generous God is to us—he makes a way for us to be with him through the giving of his Son, and he gives us gifts to share with God's people. How can you share something God has generously given you with someone else—a gift, a meal, a word from the Lord, and your prayers?

God Judges & Restores

This week we find Israel in idolatrous sin that jeopardizes the primary goal of the exodus—God's revealed presence among his people. Yet God's mercy is most visible when judgment is most deserved. He judges Israel, restores her, and promises his abiding presence. We see a clear picture of the God who will bear the guilt of his people, grant righteousness, and enable our obedience in Christ. Sister, God's gracious presence is our distinction and peace. There's good news for us this week!

EXODUS 32-34

READ
Exodus 32

IDENTIFY

How are you tempted to "Christianize" your sins?

Do you ever hide a cherished idol under the cover of sound theology or good deeds? How is Jesus your hope at these times?

I enjoyed reading several biographies this year. One of the most interesting was Frederick Douglass's *Narrative of the Life of Frederick Douglass, an American Slave*. Douglass wrote his classic autobiography to detail his enslavement, covert education, and eventual escape to the North. The book includes Douglass's rebuke of the false religiosity of his slave masters. Douglass, who professed belief in Christ as a youth, despised proclamations of faith with no evidence. He wrote,

> I am filled with unutterable loathing when I contemplate the religious pomp and show, together with the horrible inconsistencies, which every where surround me. We have men-stealers for ministers, women-whippers for missionaries, and cradle-plunderers for church members. The man who wields the blood-clotted cowskin during the week fills pulpit on Sunday, and claims to be a minister of the meek and lowly Jesus.[1]

A person can profess faith in God while drastically living in rebellion to God's teachings. We see something like this in our study today. Pressured by Israel, Aaron will sound pious as he blasphemes his Redeemer.

Our narrator turns our attention from the top of Sinai—where God conferenced with Moses—to the foot of the mountain. The scene change finds an impatient Israel. Moses had been gone for forty long days, and his delay made the people restless. They confronted Aaron with a demand: "Up, make us gods who shall go before us. As for this Moses, the man who brought us up out of the land of Egypt, we do not know what has become of him" (Exodus 32:1). God had redeemed Israel to be his covenant people. He had given moral laws to instruct them in holiness and was providing plans for his residence among them. At the same time, Aaron—the man who was to be the high priest of God's sanctuary—was collecting gold to carve an idol.

God had spoken directly to Israel at the foot of Mount Sinai: "You shall not make for yourself a carved image, or any likeness of anything that is in heaven above, or that is in the earth beneath, or that is in the water under the earth" (Exodus 20:4). Aaron heard this command, and he still took an engraving tool in one hand and the gold God had plundered from Egypt in his other hand. He fashioned a golden calf (a common symbol in Egypt).[2] Pleased with Aaron's work, the Israelites praised the image for their redemption. When Aaron saw this, he picked up his tools again to build an altar—he then scheduled a feast to *Yahweh* (Exodus 32:4-5). Aaron attempted to "clean up" Israel's idolatry with elements of true worship. The people offered burnt offerings to the Lord—and then they rose up to indulge in sin (Exodus 32:6).

A priest-elect who fashions an idol is a clear example of false virtue. You and I may be innocent of Aaron's treachery, but the apostle Paul uses him to warn us in 1 Corinthians 10:7: "Do not be idolaters as some of them were; as it is written, 'The people sat down to eat and drink and rose up to play.'" Sister, we too can "Christianize" our idolatry. We can hide our cherished sins under the cover of our religious words and deeds. We might even worship a person or a possession with a devotion we call "Christian faithfulness." Paul reminds us that Israel's failings were written for our example (1 Corinthians 10:11). We, like the Israelites, are headed to a promised city. Unlike them, we have the benefit of a sinless High Priest who turns us *away* from sin. Jesus died and rose to help us worship God alone. Let us then flee all idolatry and hypocrisy on our journey home!

CONSIDER

▶ See Exodus 32: 4–5. Israel praised the golden calf for their redemption. How did Aaron rush to "clean up" this sin with elements of true worship?

....

....

....

▶ We see in Exodus 32 that Aaron could never enter the Most Holy Place without a sacrifice to atone for his own sins. How is Jesus a High Priest of a better covenant and our hope in overcoming every sin (Hebrews 9:6–14)?

....

....

....

▶ Do you ever hide a cherished idol under the cover of sound words and deeds? Ask God to search your heart and to grant you the grace of obedience and the assurance of his ever-present help.

....

....

....

BELIEVE

He entered once for all into the holy places, not by means of the blood of goats and calves but by means of his own blood, thus securing an eternal redemption .... how much more will the blood of Christ, who through the eternal Spirit offered himself without blemish to God, purify our conscience from dead works to serve the living God.

HEBREWS 9:12, 14

READ

Exodus 32

IDENTIFY

It's not easy to confess sin. Fear of consequences and judgment might encourage denial, blaming, and evasion. What truths help to motivate your honest confession of sin when you're afraid?

Fear shows up early in the Bible. It takes hold of a man and a woman and turns them against each other. Psychologists tell us this: "When people experience overwhelming anxiety (or fear) about letting themselves or someone else down, one way to escape (flee) the perceived threatening or stressful situation is to lie, escape, or avoid."[3] We see something like this with the first man and woman in Genesis 3:8–13.

The day had grown cool when the couple heard God walking in their garden home. This sound had once delighted them, but now they scurried away. Wrapped in makeshift coverings of fig leaves and fear, the two attempted to do the impossible. They tried to hide from the presence of God. Yahweh drew them out and exposed their hearts with pointed questions:

> "Have you eaten of the tree of which I commanded you not to eat?" The man said, "The woman whom you gave to be with me, she gave me fruit of the tree, and I ate." Then the LORD God said to the woman, "What is this that you have done?" The woman said, "The serpent deceived me, and I ate." (Genesis 3:11–13)

A fallen Adam and Eve didn't confess their sin fully to God; instead, they shifted blame to another. Aaron, Israel's sovereignly elected high priest, responded in a similar way as our first parents, which we will see in today's passage.

Moses journeys down Mount Sinai where he sees a golden calf and people dancing around this graven image. His anger burned within him. Israel had broken faith with her covenant God. So, raging with anger, Moses broke the two tablets of the testimony—the commandments written with the finger of God (Exodus 32:15, 19). Next, he turned to the golden calf. Moses burned the idol "with fire and ground it to powder and scattered it on the water and made the people of Israel drink it" (Exodus 32:20). They would taste and know the bitterness of their sin (Numbers 5:18–22)—a transgression that Aaron had helped them commit.

Moses met Aaron with a hard question: "What did this people do to you that you have brought such a great sin upon them?" (Exodus 32:21). Aaron didn't respond with honest contrition but defended himself by blaming Israel: "You know the people, that they are set on evil. For they said to me, 'Make us gods who shall go before us . . . .' So I said to them, 'Let any who have gold take it off.' So, they gave it to me, and I threw it into the fire, and out came this calf" (Exodus 32:22–24). Israel's future high priest doesn't demonstrate the repentance he was called to mediate between God and his people. On the contrary, like a cornered Adam and Eve, Aaron concealed his sin and faulted others. Perhaps you've done the same?

We are the children of Adam and Eve, and our own resemblance to our first parents shows. I've been known to cover up my sins with excuses, half-truths, and blaming. Sister, if you can relate, then remember this: Christ—the Seed promised to Eve—was bruised on behalf of every covenant breaker who trusts in him (Genesis 3:15). He has suffered God's judgment for you. Therefore, "If we confess our sins, he is faithful and just to forgive us our sins and to cleanse us from all unrighteousness" (1 John. 1:9). God extends his forgiveness to you as soon as you go to him in full confession. Christ has earned that for you—there's no need to hide!

Read Numbers 5:18–22. How does Israel's drinking of bitter water point to her sin of unfaithfulness?

How does Aaron's reaction remind you of Genesis 3:8–13? How do both narratives scream out for the promised Seed of the Woman? How is he the hope of every sinner?

Praise God for the Son who suffered God's judgment on your behalf. Pray for grace to remember this good news as you confess your sins fully to God and to others.

BELIEVE

If we confess our sins, he is faithful and just to forgive us our sins and to cleanse us from all unrighteousness.

1 JOHN 1:9

READ

Exodus 33

IDENTIFY

God's personal presence is a distinguishing mark of the church. Whether in joy or pain, how does God's abiding personal presence distinguish *you* from the world?

Joni Eareckson Tada, a quadriplegic, tells a story of seeing God's presence through one traumatic incident. Tada had been invited to speak at a graduation ceremony. She was anticipating the event as her husband Ken drove her to the airport. Unfortunately, their commute would be dramatic. A vehicle veered in front of the couple's car, and Ken was forced to hit the brakes. The violent stop ejected Tada from her wheelchair, sending her to the floor. Quadriplegia kept Tada from feeling the pain of the impact. She and Ken checked her body for signs of injury. Seeing none, she boarded her flight. But after she arrived at her destination, she discovered that she had a broken leg.

Joni Eareckson Tada asked God for a song as doctors worked to reset her fractured leg. The hymn "I'm Pressing on the Upward Way" instantly came to mind. Desperate for the assurance of God's presence, Tada sang and hummed the tune from the emergency room to her speaking engagement the next day. She was shocked as the audience stood to sing that very hymn that morning. Tada concludes her story with this reminder: "God will always give you an assurance of his presence .... Today, if you are facing hardship or heartache, ask God to open your eyes to recognize the many ways he draws near to you."[4]

Friend, whether we're in suffering or in joy, God's abiding presence distinguishes his people from the remainder of those in the world. Moses affirms the same in today's passage.

We are God's people in Christ, and his personal presence is our distinctness and our peace.

God judges Israel today for her idolatry at Mount Sinai. He sent "a plague on the people, because they made the calf, the one that Aaron made" (Exodus 32:35). Many Israelites died, but God showed mercy, preserving a majority to journey onward to the promised land. Yahweh didn't change his plan to settle Israel in a homeland. He said this to Moses: "Depart; go up from here, you and the people whom you have brought up out of the land of Egypt, to the land of which I swore to Abraham, Isaac, and Jacob, saying, 'To your offspring I will give it'" (Exodus 33:1). God would keep his promise to Abraham, but he intended to withdraw his presence from his people.

God continued: "I will send an angel before you .... Go up to a land flowing with milk and honey; but I will not go up among you, lest I consume you on the way, for you are a stiff-necked people" (Exodus 33:2). The promise of a rich and fertile land still stood. However, an *angel* would guide Israel to the land—not God's personal presence. Yahweh would distance himself so that his righteous judgment doesn't swallow his people. The Israelites mourned when they heard this disastrous news. God had been with them to feed, water, protect, and guide them. The inheritance of land without the personal presence of God missed the central point of the Exodus—the personal revelation of God himself.

Sister, God's presence is throughout his creation—and yet his *personal* presence abides with his people (Psalm 139:7-12). Moses understood this and pled with God, saying, "Is it not in your going with us, so that we are distinct, I and your people, from every other people on the face of the earth?" (Exodus 33:15-16). Israel's distinctness among the nations wasn't found in her possession of a promised land alone but in God's abiding and sustaining presence. The same is true for you and me. We are God's people in Christ, and his personal presence is our distinctness and our peace.

We, like Old Testament Israel, are often a stiff-necked people who sin against God in many ways. Still, our Father will not withdraw his presence from us *because* Jesus has borne God's consuming wrath on our behalf (Isaiah 53:5; Romans 5:8-9). Our Redeemer remains to lead and sustain us on our pilgrimage to a greater promised land. Dear Sister, whether today brings you hardships or joy, know that God goes with you as you press on to higher ground!

CONSIDER

▶ How does Moses plead for mercy in today's passage? According to him, what distinguishes Israel from all other nations?

▶ Read Isaiah 53:5 and Romans 5:8–9. How does Jesus's sacrificial death remove the threat of God's wrath and thus the threat of his distance from his people?

▶ Does God's abiding personal presence distinguish you from unbelieving neighbors, friends, and family? Pray that the way you suffer *and* rejoice would testify to God's personal presence in your life.

BELIEVE

And he said, "My presence will go with you, and I will give you rest." And he said to him, "If your presence will not go with me, do not bring us up from here. For how shall it be known that I have found favor in your sight, I and your people? Is it not in your going with us, so that we are distinct, I and your people, from every other people on the face of the earth?"

EXODUS 33:14-16

READ

Exodus 34

IDENTIFY

Could you describe God to someone else? Where would you start? Here we read God's own description of himself.

Meditate on how God's description is foundational to the good news of Jesus Christ.

I wrote an essay about God as a sophomore in college. I was a new convert to Christianity and my zeal for Christ and boldness to share the gospel were overwhelming. So when my English professor gave the assignment to write a descriptive paper on any topic, it seemed like an excellent chance to introduce her to the nature and work of God. The idea was well-intentioned, but the work itself was clumsy.

My paper is long gone, and I don't remember its details. But I know that as a young Christian with little church experience and no seminary training, I found it difficult to balance the reality of God's mercy with his justice. I might cringe to read my essay now. However, the same assignment might still be difficult today. After all, how do we condense *everything* the Bible says about God into one essay? Should we leave certain points unsaid while emphasizing other characteristics of God's nature? How should we handle these questions in our face-to-face conversations? How should we describe God to others in our homes and communities? Our passage today provides some answers.

Moses is found hiking up Mount Sinai again as Exodus 34 begins. God summoned him to renew his covenant commitment with his sinful people. Israel had violated her covenant vows to Yahweh—like a fickle bride (Exodus 19:8). Yet, her Redeemer was ever faithful. God's presence would remain with the Israelites to grant them rest (Exodus 33:14). The Lord asked Moses to cut two tablets of stone like the first ones Moses had broken. Yahweh would write his commandments on stone once more as a sign of his covenant renewal. Moses rose early to scale Mount Sinai with two tablets in hand. Yahweh descended in a cloud to meet him. He passed before Moses and proclaimed,

> "The LORD, the LORD, a God merciful and gracious, slow to anger, and abounding in steadfast love and faithfulness, keeping steadfast love for thousands, forgiving iniquity and transgression and sin, but who will by no means clear the guilty, visiting the iniquity of the fathers on the children and the children's children, to the third and the fourth generation." (Exodus 34:6–7)

These verses are essential to the Bible's teaching on God's nature. This is who God is— according to God! The Lord paints his own biographical sketch with few words. He didn't give Moses a multipage essay, but he offered a succinct outline of his nature and work. God's speech is brief, and yet it is packed with revelation: the Lord is a merciful and gracious God who forgives sin but will by no means clear the guilty. This is the God who rescued Israel to make himself known to her. The Israelites were redeemed from bondage for covenant relationship with a God who would display his righteous judgment *and* merciful forgiveness toward her. Sister, God's self-description in Exodus 34:6–7 is foundational to our understanding of the gospel!

God's mercy and justice meet ultimately in Christ. The Judge who will by no means clear the guilty showed stunning grace and steadfast love to sinners when he delivered his own Son to death for our trespasses and raised him to life for our justification (Romans 4:25). God reveals his nature perfectly through Christ—and it doesn't take an essay to tell others about his unwavering justice *and* his glorious mercy. Sister, this is our God! Like Moses, our response ought to be worship.

How does God describe himself to Moses in Exodus 34:6–7? Who is God, according to God?

How does God reveal his nature perfectly through Christ? How do we see his unwavering justice *and* glorious mercy through the death and resurrection of his Son?

Are you tempted to omit some aspects of God's character when sharing him with others? Pray for grace to see God clearly though the lens of the gospel. Worship the righteous Judge who grants mercy through Christ.

BELIEVE

The LORD passed before him and proclaimed, "The LORD, the LORD, a God merciful and gracious, slow to anger, and abounding in steadfast love and faithfulness, keeping steadfast love for thousands, forgiving iniquity and transgression and sin, but who will by no means clear the guilty, visiting the iniquity of the fathers on the children and the children's children, to the third and the fourth generation."

E X O D U S   3 4 : 6 - 7

READ

Exodus 34

IDENTIFY

Today we get a glimpse of how God's glory transforms his people. What an amazing picture for us as we live day by day in an inglorious world. The unfading glory of the new covenant is ours— it gives us courage for our lives and fuels our boldness in sharing the hope we have in Christ.

The Lion, the Witch, and the Wardrobe is the first of seven books in C. S. Lewis's Chronicles of Narnia. The final title in the series is *The Last Battle*. This book concludes the adventures of the Pevensie children, with the death of Peter, Edmund, and Lucy. Narnia itself dies in this book as well.

The children enter a new and eternal Narnia (Aslan's *true* country), and from there, they watch the de-creation of the first Narnia. Aslan invites them to journey "further up and further in" to a splendid new world. We see that the glory of the temporary Narnia was a mere dream and a shadow compared to the glory of the eternal Narnia. Lewis closes the book with these words: "All their adventures in Narnia had only been the cover and the title page; now at last they were beginning Chapter One of the Great Story."[5]

In many ways, our passage today is like the title page to a greater coming chapter in the story of redemption. The glory we see in Exodus 34 is only a shadow of the later glory God would reveal to his people. Our study begins with Moses standing before God on Mount Sinai.

Moses stayed on Mount Sinai for forty days and forty nights as God wrote his laws, the Ten Commandments, on tablets of stone for his covenant community (Exodus 34:28). Moses would descend this mountain transformed. Exodus 34:30 says, "Aaron and all the people of Israel saw Moses, and behold, the skin of his face shone, and they were afraid to come near him." God's reflected glory clung to Moses after his extended meeting with Yahweh. Israel fled from Moses, just as she had retreated from God back in Exodus 20:18-21. Moses reassured the people, and they grew calm enough to draw near to him. He repeated God's law and covenant obligations, and then he did something perplexing: Moses put a veil over his face (Exodus 34:33).

I used to think that Moses shrouded his face behind a veil as a response to the people's fears. However, a careful notice of the text proves otherwise. We read in Exodus 34:34-35 that Moses covered his face whenever he *finished* addressing Israel:

> Whenever Moses went in before the Lord to speak with him, he would remove the veil, until he came out. And when he came out and told the people of Israel what he was commanded, the people of Israel would see the face of Moses, that the skin of Moses' face was shining. And Moses would put the veil over his face again, until he went in to speak with him.

The apostle Paul helps us understand this passage in 2 Corinthians 3:13. Paul explains that while Moses's face shone with the glory of God, it was a *fading* glory. Israel's mediator concealed his face to keep the nation from seeing the vanishing radiance. This temporary glory signified the passing glory of the old covenant. The covenant at Sinai would be replaced by a better covenant with an unfading glory (2 Corinthians 3:7-13)!

Sister, the Spirit of the living God is given to you who are in Christ. This means that you experience the glorious ministry of the Spirit in a way that old covenant saints never did. Moses's passing glory cannot compare to the glory God reflects through Christ's church. The Spirit writes God's law on the tablet of *your* heart—not on tablets of stones. He enables your obedience of God's Word. And far from fading, he is ever transforming you to boldly reflect the glorious image of Christ to the world (2 Corinthians 3:18). Sister, there's no need to hide behind a veil! Share your hope with others as you journey further up and further in to God's already (but still to come) eternal kingdom!

CONSIDER

▶ Why did Moses put a veil over his face (2 Corinthians 3:12–13)? How does this signify the temporary and insufficient nature of the Mosaic covenant?

....

....

....

....

▶ What's one way the Holy Spirit enables your obedience to God's commandments (see 2 Corinthians 3:3)? How does this distinguish the new covenant in Christ from the old Mosaic covenant?

....

....

....

....

▶ Read 2 Corinthians 3:12. Does the unfading glory of the new covenant fuel your hope and boldness in Christ? Pray for unfading boldness as you share gospel hope with others!

....

....

....

....

BELIEVE

For if what was being brought to an end came with glory, much more will what is permanent have glory. Since we have such a hope, we are very bold.

2 CORINTHIANS 3:11-12

Take
&
Share

We started this week thinking about all the ways we go wrong and how God exposes our sins, and we end by thinking about shining with God's glory. This is the gospel! God tells us the truth about our need for him and provides his one and only Son to die in our place so we can be forgiven. This is news worth sharing with everyone you know! Who can you talk to about Jesus today?

God Prepares

The story of Exodus will soon conclude. God extends his forgiveness, and the nation turns from her sins to loving obedience of God as she takes the tabernacle from a plan to an actual structure. We are encouraged this week to work faithfully for the Lord in our own labors. As you do, know that the One who will ultimately inspect your work for loving obedience has also asked his Father to give you a Helper— the Spirit of the living God.

EXODUS 35-39

READ
Exodus 35

IDENTIFY

We live in the "age of apology." Expressions of regret are easy and common. How is your Christian repentance distinct from this kind of worldly sorrow or apology?

I grew up in an immigrant community with an older generation of people who didn't often apologize. It was rare to hear the words "I'm sorry" from adults around me. It can be painful to live with a stubborn impenitent individual, but the same can be said for the person who expresses an insincere remorse. In other words, an empty apology is just as terrible as a refusal to apologize. Statements of regret are abundant today in the broader American society. Unfortunately, these remarks often sound shallow. The *Throughline Podcast* describes our "age of apology" like this:

> Our society is saturated in apologies. They're scripted, they're public, and they often feel less than sincere. Political, corporate, celebrity apologies—they can all feel performed. It's not even always clear who they're for. So, what purpose do these apologies serve? Because real apologies are not just PR stunts. Not just a way to move on. At their best, they're about acknowledgment and accountability, healing and repair.[1]

Our apology-soaked culture has come to see an important truth: a genuine "sorry" is proved more by changed behavior than the crafting of words. This should make sense to Christians who are called not only to grief and remorse, but to *repentance*. Israel gives us a glimpse of genuine repentance in our present passage.

The building of the tabernacle begins today, and with it comes a refreshing response from Israel. Moses turned Israel's attention to the construction of the tabernacle after God's covenant renewal. He assembled the nation and said,

> "This is the thing that the LORD has commanded. Take from among you a contribution to the LORD. Whoever is of a generous heart, let him bring the LORD's contribution: gold, silver, and bronze . . . " (Exodus 35:4–5)

These precious metals—along with gifts of yarn, wood, oil, and precious stones—would be used to build the tabernacle precisely as Yahweh had instructed. Moses gave the charge and the people listened, then departed for their tents. They would reemerge looking very different from the nation we've known.

The Israelites reassembled with their contributions in hand. The group must have included a sizable portion of women because the narrator spotlights their presence: "All the women whose hearts stirred them to use their skill spun the goats' hair. . . . All the men and women, the people of Israel, whose heart moved them to bring anything for the work that the Lord had commanded by Moses to be done brought it as a freewill offering to the Lord" (Exodus 35:26–29). Israel has continuously faltered in faith throughout their Exodus journey with God. We get a different picture in Exodus 35. The idolatrous nation who offered their gold and worship to an idol now contributed their treasures and talents to God's construction work. Men and women together turned away from their former sins to turn toward God. Here we find godly repentance acted out beautifully.

Friend, Christians are commanded to *repent* from sin, not merely to regret it. According to the apostle Paul, to grieve sin without repentance is to resemble the world (2 Corinthians 7:10). Politicians, corporations, celebrities, and some in our community might use apologies as public relations stunts, but not so with God's people. Our grief over sin must be the godly kind that produces repentance and change. We turn from going our own way to going God's way. That means that we flee from our sin and move toward God. And here's some good news: we don't run alone. The Spirit of God enables us to demonstrate a repentance that leads to life. Sister, God's Spirit is with us, and we can do even better than the women at Sinai. We can bring more than freewill offerings; we can repent with our whole hearts.

CONSIDER

▶ How is Israel's behavior in Exodus 35 distinct from her behavior in Exodus 32? How does she use her treasures in both chapters?

....

....

....

....

▶ Read 2 Corinthians 7:9–12. How does the apostle distinguish between godly grief and worldly grief? How is Christian repentance distinct from worldly remorse?

....

....

....

....

▶ How does godly grief look different from worldly remorse in your own life? Pray that the Spirt would enable Christians to demonstrate true repentance from sin in our "age of apology."

....

....

....

....

BELIEVE

For godly grief produces a repentance that leads to salvation without regret, whereas worldly grief produces death.

2 CORINTHIANS 7:10

READ

Exodus 35

IDENTIFY

We live in a culture that values ambition and honors certain roles above others. Whatever your job, what inspires you to work faithfully, as for the Lord and not for men?

I'm not always sure how to respond to that infamous question, "What do you do?" As an at-home mom (who writes and teaches on the side), I rarely feel prepared to give an answer. I greet my smiling interrogator with a momentary pause. My mind feels blank—yet, at the same time crowded with tiny snapshots of the many things I do throughout the day. I see myself cooking, cleaning, writing, chasing a toddler, preparing Bible lessons to teach women, and instructing my homeschooled daughters. Which of these activities is this person asking me to talk about? Which of my many jobs should I set before her as the "right answer"?

My awkward reaction to the question of what I do is common to other women—especially those who care for children at home. Lisa Endlich Heffernan explains it well:

> The question, "What do you do?" really means, "What do you do *besides* look after your family, clean your house, grocery shop, and volunteer in your community?" The question touches on our identity and ambition, how others value us, and even how our children perceive us. The question asks, "What does someone pay you to do?" And for that, I had no answer.[2]

The evolving seasons of a woman's life can bring various jobs at various times. Our work tends to ebb and flow with the tide of changing commitments and priorities. A woman might hold many roles within a lifetime. Whatever the story, we are called to work heartily, as for the Lord (Colossians 3:23). The craftsmen in today's passage provide such an example.

Moses received Israel's contributions for the tabernacle construction and then moved on to choosing craftsman to do the work. The costly materials for the labor had ultimately come from God (we've noted how Yahweh plundered the Egyptians back in Exodus 12:36). Now God would also supply a building crew. Moses explained,

> "See, the Lord has called by name Bezalel the son of Uri, son of Hur, of the tribe of Judah; and he has filled him with the Spirit of God, with skill, with intelligence, with knowledge, and with all craftsmanship, to devise artistic designs, to work in gold and silver and bronze." (Exodus 35:30–32)

God had revealed his intention to fill Bezalel with his Spirit and with skill back on Mount Sinai. That day was in sight.

God's Spirit would soon empower Bezalel, along with Oholiab, for the task. In addition, the Spirit would inspire these men to instruct others in their craft (Exodus 35:34). Beginning with the design of the tabernacle to the metal engravings to the embroidery of curtains to the mixing of incense, Bezalel, Oholiab, and the craftsmen of Israel would build the tabernacle precisely as God had ordered. They would work heartily, as for the Lord.

We live in a culture that values ambition and honors certain roles above others. Some of us will answer the question of what we do easier than others. Sister, whatever your response, remember that some Christians are called to formal ministry work and others to various industries and trades. In each case, Christ has given the Spirit to help his church serve with "sincerity of heart, fearing the Lord" (Colossians 3:22). You may be a doctor, a campus ministry worker, or an at-home mom, but "Whatever you do, work heartily, as for the Lord and not for men" (Colossians 3:23). The answer to the question of how you lived your days belongs ultimately to God. May we answer him with joy!

CONSIDER

▶ Bezalel and Oholiab were temporarily empowered by the Spirit for a specific job. How is the ministry of the Spirit among God's people more than a temporary indwelling today (see John 16:4–15)?

....

....

....

....

▶ Do you find it difficult to answer the question, "What do you do?" Why or why not?

....

....

....

....

▶ Whatever you do, pray for the grace to work heartily, as for the Lord and not for men. Who can you ask to pray for/with you if you're struggling with your work/role in your current season?

....

....

....

....

BELIEVE

Whatever you do, work heartily, as for the Lord and not for men.

C O L O S S I A N S   3 : 2 3

READ

Exodus 37:1–9

IDENTIFY

Some parts of the Bible can seem repetitive and boring. How can even these portions of Scripture reveal our Redeemer to us?

Do you believe that *all* Scripture is profitable for your instruction?

I'm a homeschool mom who teaches writing to elementary-school-aged daughters. I've edited countless fourth through sixth grade papers and have noticed that it is common practice among my developing writers to repeat themselves a lot. My students recycle their words, phrases, and ideas. They might sprinkle the same transitional word, like *also*, throughout their work or write a sentence that duplicates the one just before it. Grading these papers has taught me that pointless repetition can frustrate and bore the reader. Yet, repetition as a literary-controlled tool has its benefits. Just look at the writing of Dr. Seuss:

> "Left foot, left foot,
> Right foot, right.
> Feet in the morning,
> Feet in the night."[3]

Repetition is common in children's literature. When done as brilliantly as Dr. Seuss, humorous and memorable words delight and instruct the reader. For instance, the above lines from Dr. Seuss's *The Foot Book* could be used to teach a child to differentiate between their two feet. A good teacher will repeat herself for emphasis and memory, and it's always wise to note what a good teacher repeats. We find repetitions in our passage today that point beautifully to the gospel.

It's wise to pay
attention to what
God repeats.
And wise to
repeat it to yourself
and others.

Bezalel and his crew begin the official construction of the tabernacle. Moses reports the event like a storyteller who is repurposing his earlier material. He alludes back to earlier chapters. Exodus 37–39 matches closely with chapters 25–31. Some may question Moses's linguistic use of repetition here, asking, "Isn't he risking the frustration and boredom of his audience by rehearsing details written elsewhere? Is this the best writing the Bible can offer?" Friend, if you and others you know have wrestled with this question, then rest assured that God isn't some weak writer who repeats himself for nothing. What he restates is meant for your notice—and for your good. Consider one example from Exodus 37:1–9.

We find a repeated description of the mercy seat as Bezalel begins his work today. The mercy seat, a rectangular structure made of pure gold, sat on top of the ark and was adorned with two winged cherubim on either end (Exodus 25:17–21; 37:6–9). Moses spotlights the mercy seat for its significance: God would meet with Israel from between the two cherubim (Exodus 25:22).

The New Testament alludes to this structure with a new and glorious emphasis: In John's account of the resurrection, a weeping Mary Magdalene searches Jesus's tomb to find "two angels in white, sitting where the body of Jesus had lain, one at the head and one at the feet" (John 20:11–12). As R. C. Sproul mentions, the position of these angels (one at either end of where Jesus had lain) takes us back to Exodus 25 and 37.[4]

Friend, in Christ, the God who met with Israel between the cherubim showed his greatest act of mercy. He sent his Son from the Holy of Holies to live, die, and rise for our redemption!

Sister, the Bible is one big story with unfolding themes that meet their fulfillment in Christ. You may know neighbors and friends who meet the Bible's repetitive sections with frustration and boredom. But God's people know better. We believe that all Scripture (even the repeated parts) is "breathed out by God and profitable for teaching, for reproof, for correction, and for training in righteousness" (2 Timothy 3:16). Good teachers repeat themselves for emphasis. They purposefully rehearse vital information for the sake of memory and instruction. So it's wise to pay attention to what God repeats. And wise to repeat it to yourself and others.

CONSIDER

▶ Notice references to Israel's exodus throughout the Bible (Psalm 114; Daniel 9:15; Habakkuk 3). Why do you think the Bible continues to reference this event?

▶ The Bible is one big story with unfolding themes that meet their fulfillment in Christ. Do you struggle to see how certain portions of Scripture contribute to that big story? Why or why not?

▶ Do you believe that all Scripture is breathed out by God and profitable for your instruction? Pray for the grace to see God's wisdom in how he's written his Word (seek resources that can help you do this well).

BELIEVE

All Scripture is breathed out by God and profitable for teaching, for reproof, for correction, and for training in righteousness.

2 TIMOTHY 3:16

READ

Exodus 39

IDENTIFY

It can feel shameful to turn back to God after sinning. Yet, his forgiveness isn't stingy and he doesn't hold grudges. How is God's compassion greater than your sins?

The Bible connects the themes of forgiveness and clothing in a few places. One of these is found in the parable of the Prodigal Son, which was told in Luke 15:11–32. The younger son of a certain man requested his share of his father's property. The boy left home for a faraway country, and there, he squandered his money in reckless living. A famine hit the land just as he lost his funds and friends. Destitute and alone, the young man hired himself out as a pig tender. The boy came to his senses when he found the pigs' meals better than his own. He decided to turn his feet toward the direction of his father's house. His journey would end with a great surprise.

The young man believed that he was no longer worthy to be called a son in his father's home. He prepared a speech asking for forgiveness and a job as a servant.

> But while he was still a long way off, his father saw him and felt compassion, and ran and embraced him and kissed him . . . . The father said to his servants, "Bring quickly the best robe, and put it on him, and put a ring on his hand, and shoes on his feet" (Luke 15:20–22).

Friend, the father in this parable is meant to represent a

greater Father who covers his repentant children with generous grace. We can see that in today's passage from Exodus.

In Exodus 39, God's plan to clothe his priests in beautiful, meaningful garments unfolds. Exodus 39:1 is shocking in view of Exodus 32. God gave forgiveness and restoration to the man who had fashioned a golden calf for Israel's worship. Aaron, perhaps fearing the Israelites, brazenly extended his hands to receive their gold ornaments. He then designed a calf that Israel welcomed with these words: "These are your gods, O Israel, who brought you up out of the land of Egypt!" (Exodus 32:4). But none of that would stop God from designing and fashioning holy garments for Aaron. In this chapter, Aaron comes into focus again as Bezalel and his craftsmen begin sewing priestly vestments.

Like Aaron before him, Bezalel extended his hands and took Israel's contributions of gold and costly materials. He would use these to make a breastpiece, an ephod (a vestlike garment), robe, coat, turban, sash, and undergarments for Aaron. Bezalel hammered out gold leaf to shape the ephod. He took blue, purple, and scarlet yarns, along with fine twined linen, and worked these skillfully into the ephod. He then crafted a breastpiece set with twelve precious stones. Next, he weaved a blue robe lined with linen pomegranates and golden bells on its hem. The coat, turban, undergarments, and sash were embroidered with needlework and woven of fine twined linen and of blue, purple, and scarlet yarns. Bezalel then made the turban. He inscribed the words "Holy to the Lord" on a pure gold plate and fastened it to Aaron's turban (v. 30). God would clothe his high priest in glory and in beauty (Exodus 28:2).

We are all sinners who fall short in our obedience to God. Our prodigal moments can be as fleeting as a lie told in fear or as dramatic as some hidden habitual sin. Sister, the God who clothed a fallen Adam and Eve in the garden (Genesis 3:21) and who dressed a sinful Aaron at Sinai runs to cover every sinner who comes to him in repentance. Know that your Father's forgiveness isn't stingy, and he doesn't hold grudges. Jesus Christ, his Son, was dressed to be mocked (Matthew 27:28) and then bore your shame on the cross (Hebrews 12:2), so that he could clothe you forever in beauty and glory (Revelation 19:8). He will clothe you in robes of righteousness (Isaiah 61:10). Whatever your sin, the moment it comes to mind, turn to the Father whose compassion is greater than your sins.

CONSIDER

▶ God ordained Aaron's clothing in Exodus 28—before his Exodus 32 idolatry. How does Exodus 39 demonstrate God's forgiveness toward sinners?

....

....

....

▶ What does the Bible's theme of clothing say about God's gracious mercy? Consider Genesis 3:21 and Luke 15:11–32.

....

....

....

▶ Are you kept away from God by carrying a weight of shame after sinning? Ask God to help you see him as the compassionate Father who stands ready to clothe you in his grace.

....

....

....

....

BELIEVE

"And he arose and came to his father. But while he was still a long way off, his father saw him and felt compassion, and ran and embraced him and kissed him. And the son said to him, 'Father, I have sinned against heaven and before you. I am no longer worthy to be called your son.' But the father said to his servants, 'Bring quickly the best robe, and put it on him, and put a ring on his hand, and shoes on his feet.'"

LUKE 15:20-22

READ

Exodus 39

IDENTIFY

Have you ever wondered, What's the best love gift I could give to Christ? Remember that he has already given the answer—your obedience. What greater gift does *he* offer to help you obey him?

I once gave my husband $4 store-bought cookies for Christmas. The gift was cheap but not random. It was a pack of Stella D'oro Swiss fudge cookies—and I knew it would make him smile. My husband is a New Yorker who grew up in the '80s and early-'90s. Stella D'oro cookies were popular during his childhood. He ate many and watched endless advertisements about them. He mentioned one nostalgic commercial to me about a month before Christmas, so I viewed the ad on YouTube.[5]

The commercial portrays a husband's attempt to give his wife the perfect gift. The woman drops numerous hints for Stella D'oro cookies, but her husband ignores her, preferring something more lavish. He brings home a diamond ring, then a gold watch and pearls. The wife is polite but unimpressed. She doesn't brighten up until her husband hands her a pack of Stella D'oro Swiss fudge cookies. She is delighted in the simple gift that said, "I'm listening to you." Our passage today shows Israel giving God his expressed desire—simply her obedience.

Israel completes the construction of the tabernacle and its furnishings in chapter 39 of our study. The people brought their work to Moses for inspection. Like a faithful project manager who must give an account to a higher-level boss, Moses stepped forward to appraise *everything* God had commanded Israel to build. His checklist was extensive. Consider the grand inventory of items detailed in Exodus 39:33–41:

> The tent [of the tabernacle] and all its utensils, its hooks, its frames, its bars, its pillars, and its bases; the covering of tanned rams' skins and goatskins, and the veil of the screen; the ark of the testimony with its poles and the mercy seat; the table with all its utensils, and the bread of the Presence; the lampstand of pure gold and its lamps with the lamps set and all its utensils, and the oil for the light; the golden altar, the anointing oil and the fragrant incense, and the screen for the entrance of the tent; the bronze altar, and its grating of bronze, its poles, and all its utensils; the basin and its stand; the hangings of the court, its pillars, and its bases, and the screen for the gate of the court, its cords, and its pegs; and all the utensils for the service of the tabernacle, for the tent of meeting; the finely worked garments for ministering in the Holy Place, the holy garments for Aaron the priest, and the garments of his sons for their service as priests.

God had given Israel a big job! With a large task comes many opportunities for complaints and slips. Yet Moses found everything finished according to God's commandments. Considering Israel's history of grumbling and rebellion, Exodus 39:43 is sweet: "And Moses saw all the work, and behold, they had done it; as the Lord had commanded, so had they done it. Then Moses blessed them." Israel had vowed her obedience to God earlier in this book (Exodus 19:8; 24:3). Here we see actual obedience that God blesses!

The evidence of our love for God isn't found in our oral professions of allegiance but in obedience that our Redeemer is pleased to bless (Deuteronomy 28:1–2). You don't have to search for some extravagant way to demonstrate your affections for Christ; he has already told you what he wants: "If you love me, you will keep my commandments" (John 14:15). And his commands are simple—love God and love your neighbor. And if those simple commands feel impossible, remember what he says next: "And I will ask the Father, and he will give you another Helper, to be with you forever" (John 14:16). Dear Sister, the One who will ultimately inspect your works for loving obedience has given you the best gift ever—his own Spirit to help you!

CONSIDER

▶ Why does Moses bless Israel in Exodus 39:43? How does this act of blessing point forward to God's promise to his people in Deuteronomy 28:1–2?

▶ Jesus's promise of a Helper comes immediately after his command for loving obedience. How is John 14:16 an encouragement to you on days when John 14:15 feels difficult?

▶ Thank God for the gift of his Spirit, your ever-present Helper. Ask him to empower your loving obedience to Christ today!

BELIEVE

"If you love me, you will keep my commandments. And I will ask the Father, and he will give you another Helper, to be with you forever."

JOHN 14:15-16

Take & Share

This is a beautiful section of Scripture, full of promised blessings for all who turn to God through Christ in repentance and faith. We find here that we are forgiven, welcomed, and clothed by our Savior Jesus who died so all of these blessings could be ours. Then we get the joy of living a life of obedient love. Who do can you share this good news with today?

God Dwells

We've reached the climactic conclusion of our journey! God has redeemed Israel from Egypt to dwell with his covenant people. His glory fills the completed tabernacle, and we get a backward glimpse of Eden. At the same time, we catch a foreshadowing of the future—a new creation with a redeemed humanity, sanctified to live with God forever. Sister, Jesus is preparing that new creation right now, and his Spirit is getting you ready for it! Your part is to cooperate, trusting his Word as your faithful guide to that kingdom that is here—yet still ahead.

EXODUS 40

READ

Exodus
40:1–8

IDENTIFY

We often view
Jesus's work of
salvation in past and
future tenses—but
what is he doing for
his church *right now*?

How can Jesus's
work on this ordinary
day encourage your
heart?

As newlyweds, my husband, Eric, and I stayed in the home
of a couple we had never met before. We were invited to
a wedding in Lancaster, Pennsylvania. The groom-to-be
was born in that town. He wanted to spare wedding guests
the cost of a hotel room and asked his community to host
his friends. Eric and I have never forgotten the remarkable
hospitality of the family we stayed with. The couple had re-
tired from full-time employment and now worked to host
people in their home for free. They took that job seriously
and prepared carefully for their guests. From their greeting
at the door, to our meals, to our room, to the toiletries
they offered, this couple treated strangers like family.

We find Moses and Israel working to assemble a "room"
for Yahweh in today's passage. Our study of Exodus 40 will
also point us to another host who is presently working to
welcome his many guests.

Exodus 40 marks nine months since Israel arrived at
Mount Sinai.[1] The nation had experienced both highs and
lows at the foot of that mountain. Nine months later, they
were on the verge of something new. God told Moses to
erect the tabernacle on the first day of the first month of

the new year (Exodus 40:1). The various parts of the tabernacle were ready. But like online furniture that comes unassembled, Israel had to put the full structure together. God had designed and guided the construction of the tabernacle. Now he would give Moses the assembly instructions. God's directions began with the Most Holy Place—his throne room.

Yahweh said to Moses, "You shall erect the tabernacle of the tent of meeting. And you shall put in it the ark of the testimony, and you shall screen the ark with the veil" (Exodus 40:1-2). The ark of the testimony would sit behind the veil in the Most Holy Place. God would meet with Israel at that ark—more precisely at the mercy seat above the ark. It was made of pure gold with two cherubs on either end—wings spread and outward facing (Exodus 25:21-22). The mercy seat was a symbol for God's throne. Moses began his assembly work by putting together the seat and the room from which God would commune with Israel. Moses's preparations here recall one unique role of the ascended Lord Jesus.

We commonly view Jesus's saving work in past and future tenses. In other words, he bore our judgment in the past and will return to make all things new in the future. We think less often about his *current* work on our behalf. Simply put, what is Jesus doing right now? He's doing many things, including readying a seat and a room for you in God's house. Our Lord is preparing the ultimate communion between God and his innumerable people. He shared these comforting words with his despairing disciples shortly before his crucifixion:

> "Let not your hearts be troubled. Believe in God; believe also in me. In my Father's house are many rooms. If it were not so, would I have told you that I go to prepare a place for you? And if I go and prepare a place for you, I will come again and will take you to myself, that where I am you may be also." (John 14:1-3)

Sister, Moses erected the mercy seat for God to reign among Israel. Jesus is preparing a seat for you to live forever with the God who reigns. On this ordinary day, he is ensuring a ready room and a forever place for you with God. So let not your heart be troubled. Whatever the day may bring, believe in a Mediator better than Moses. Jesus is a host who does all things well—whether they be done in the past, present, or future.

God directed the ark to be assembled first. How did the ark represent his enthroned presence among Israel (see Exodus 25:10–22)?

Read John 14:1–3. Why does Jesus's work of preparation ensure our future communion with God?

How does Jesus's work of preparation encourage your heart today? Thank God for a Mediator better than Moses and a Redeemer who is preparing a place for his church!

BELIEVE

"Let not your hearts be troubled. Believe in God; believe also in me. In my Father's house are many rooms. If it were not so, would I have told you that I go to prepare a place for you? And if I go and prepare a place for you, I will come again and will take you to myself, that where I am you may be also."

JOHN 14:1-3

READ
Exodus 40:1–15

IDENTIFY

Jesus is preparing a place for you, and his Spirit is preparing you for that place. How are you cooperating with the Spirit's work to make you holy?

Adam and Maria Kreutinger met in high school and dated for fifteen years before getting married. Their wedding itself was typical, and yet it made the local news.[2] It was unique because Adam, an art teacher, made Maria's wedding dress and veil. He designed the gown, purchased all the materials, created a mannequin from her measurements, and remained at his sewing machine for fifteen days. Maria saw the dress for the first time on their wedding day, and she wore it with joyful pride.

We don't hear many stories like that of the Kreutingers. A groom sewing his bride's dress is unusual, as is a bride relinquishing the selection and the design of her bridal gown to her fiancé. Adam's ability to serve Maria in this unique way *and* Maria's confidence in Adam's skillfulness makes their circumstance newsworthy. From their story, we gain a sweet illustration of a greater Bridegroom who is working to clothe his trusting bride. Jesus, through his Spirit, is dressing his church for eternity. Today's passage recalls that truth.

With the tabernacle assembled, the time came to get the priests ready who would minister in it. In chapter 40, God gives his final instructions for Aaron's consecration. Moses was to bring his elder brother to the entrance of the tent of meeting. There Aaron would be washed with water and cleansed before the Lord. He would wear his holy garments—made for beauty and glory—for the first time. Moses would anoint his brother and inaugurate him as Israel's high priest. The day would be a glorious one for Aaron and for his sons.

Aaron's four sons, Nadab, Abihu, Eleazar, and Ithamar, would follow their father to the entrance of the tent of meeting. They too would be cleansed with water and robed in priestly coats. Moses would anoint them to serve God as priests. The sons of Aaron would enter a perpetual priesthood to last throughout their generations. They would serve as mediators between Yahweh and his covenant people. They would cleanse Israel to meet with her God.

Yesterday, we were reminded that Jesus is currently preparing a place in heaven for his redeemed. As the Lord works in heaven, his Spirit is working on earth to prepare God's people for that place. The Holy Spirit has many roles, one of which is sanctifier. He works to make you holy from the moment of your conversion to your death. For this reason, Christ's church will stand before him one day like a bride dressed in "fine linen, bright and pure" (Revelation 19:7-8). This ministry of sanctification belongs to the Spirit alone—and yet, we are called to cooperate.

Sister, just as Aaron and his sons had to walk to the tent of meeting to be washed and clothed, so must we participate in the Spirit's work of cleansing. God uses your devotion to the Scriptures, your fellowship with the saints, your prayers, and your participation in communion to achieve his sanctifying purposes. "It is God who works in you, both to will and to work for his good pleasure" (Philippians 2:13). We have a Bridegroom who is dressing his church for eternity—and amazingly, he's using our daily lives of faith in his work!

CONSIDER

▶ Aaron's holy clothes were completed in the previous chapter, in Exodus 39:27–31. What needed to happen before he could wear them? Why is this significant?

....

....

....

▶ Jesus is preparing a place for his people. How is the Spirit of God getting God's people ready for that place?

....

....

....

▶ What does Philippians 2:12–13 say about our participation in the work of sanctification? Who empowers you to will and work? Rejoice in the One who is getting you ready for eternity.

....

....

....

BELIEVE

Therefore, my beloved, as you have always obeyed, so now, not only as in my presence but much more in my absence, work out your own salvation with fear and trembling, for it is God who works in you, both to will and to work for his good pleasure.

PHILIPPIANS 2:12-13

READ

Exodus
40:1–33

IDENTIFY

 Our life of faith often feels more like a crawl than a fast race. If you wonder how you can know you will persevere to the end, there's assurance for you.

Derek and Jim Redmond's inspirational story is the stuff of legends.[3] Derek Redmond was a British Olympic 400-meter runner. Redmond had experienced several years of injuries and setbacks in his athletic career. He had hoped to win a medal at the 1988 Olympic Games in Seoul, South Korea, but he tore his Achilles tendon only one hour before that event. Four years later, Redmond had healed, trained hard, and was ready to represent his country in the Barcelona games. Unfortunately for the runner, this race wouldn't end as planned.

Derek Redmond began the Barcelona 400-meter run in a strong position. He was in step with the pack until the race's halfway mark. Here Redmond grabbed the back of his right thigh and sank down in apparent pain. The runner had torn his hamstring. Other runners sped to the finish line as Redmond stood up and began hopping on his left foot. The stadium cheered their encouragement as he limped painfully in his lane, determined to complete the race. An unexpected second runner joined Redmond on that slow trek.

Redmond's dad, Jim, appeared to his left. The father was as determined to remain with his son as the son was to finish the race. Jim Redmond dismissed the Olympic officials who attempted to call him off the track. He held his weeping son by the waist as they walked the last meter of the race together. Derek Redmond persevered to the end, with the help of his father. We witness a version of this in our passage today.

Israel reaches her own finish line today. We find these exciting words in Exodus 40:32-33:

> When they went into the tent of meeting, and when they approached the altar, they washed, as the LORD commanded Moses. And he erected the court around the tabernacle and the altar, and set up the screen of the gate of the court. So Moses finished the work.

Moses and Israel completed everything as the Lord commanded! God's tabernacle was erected, with dressed and consecrated priests in position. Like Derek Redmond, Israel's journey to this point had not been smooth. The nation grumbled, complained, and broke covenant obligations (Exodus 17; 32). But God's presence remained with his covenant people to forgive, instruct, and sustain (Exodus 33:14). Israel persevered with the help of God.

Friend, our own journeys to glory come with bumps and falls. We fail to consider others more highly than ourselves—placing our comforts and desires above those we're called to love. And, like Israel, our trust in God gives way to grumbling and fear when we forget his demonstrated power and goodness toward us. We don't love God and neighbor perfectly. To be honest, our life of faith often feels more like a crawl than a fast race. Perhaps you wonder, *How do I know I can persevere to the end?*

Dear Sister in Christ, whether you're running or limping, you will make it home to God! Here's why: our perseverance doesn't ultimately rest on our willpower but on the God who has begun a good work in us (Philippians 1:6). Your faith was initiated by God, and he will nurture that faith until it is perfected at the coming of Christ. We are God's workmanship, and our God finishes every work that *he* begins. Sister, persevere home—leaning on the One who has already finished the race.

Your faith was initiated by God, and he will nurture that faith until it is perfected at the coming of Christ.

CONSIDER

▶ Who initiated your faith in Christ? Who will bring that faith to completion? How can Philippians 1:6 encourage you on days when your faith feels especially small?

▶ What does it look like for you to "lean on God" in your faith walk? How do Christian fellowship, prayer, and God's Word strengthen your journey with Christ?

▶ Is there a persevering sister you can encourage today? Pray for that person and reach out to her in a meaningful way.

BELIEVE

And I am sure of this, that he who began a good work in you will bring it to completion at the day of Jesus Christ.

PHILIPPIANS 1:6

READ

Exodus
40:1–35

IDENTIFY

The Bible will end as it began— and that ending has already started. Does your enjoyment of God today testify to that truth?

The biggest story ever told begins in a garden. God, a self-existent Creator, is the first and only character on the scene as the curtain rises. He made the heavens and the earth by the power of his word. He filled his created world with trees and plants, stars and celestial bodies, sea creatures, birds, and land animals. God saw his creation and called it good, but his work was not complete. The crown of his creation was yet to come. And this time, God would not only speak but also turn and fashion dust to make a creature in his own image.

"Then God said, 'Let us make man in our image, after our likeness . . . . So God created man in his own image, in the image of God he created him; male and female he created them" (Genesis 1:26–27). God's creation of the man and the woman is the climax of the creation narrative–no other creature is made in God's likeness. Adam and his wife were called to reflect God in their rule and stewardship of the world. They would tend to the fruit of the land and stock the earth with people–the fruit of the womb (Genesis

1:28). And they would do all this in the company of the Creator himself. God's visible presence would abide with his image-bearers (Genesis 3:8)! This was the reality until sin slithered into the story.

God and his image-bearers move apart as the curtain closes on the creation narrative (Genesis 3:23–24). The man and the woman would still multiply and govern the earth, but they would do so outside the garden—in a wilderness full of thorns, thistles, and torment (Genesis 3:16–19). How incredible, then, to consider Exodus 40:34–35, where God comes to tabernacle with his people in that wilderness!

God redeemed Israel from Egypt to dwell with his covenant people. We reach the climactic end of our epic journey as God's glory fills the completed and assembled tabernacle. Our passage today gives us a small glimpse of Eden—God comes to live with men and women. Exodus 40 is a stunning point in redemptive history. And still, there is a bit of tension in verse 35: "And Moses was not able to enter the tent of meeting because the cloud settled on it, and the glory of the Lord filled the tabernacle." Distance remains between the Creator and mankind as God's consuming glory overwhelms even Moses. We are reminded that the Old Testament tabernacle was only a provisional solution to a problem God would ultimately resolve through his Son.

God's intention from the beginning of Scripture was to dwell with his people. Sin separated us from God, but he never abandoned his plan. Exodus 40 reminds us of Eden, but it points forward to a day far more glorious! In time, God would send his own Son to tabernacle with his creation (John 1:1–18). Jesus, the image of the invisible God, would live sinlessly for thirty-three years and would die and rise to purchase a people for God. Christ is sanctifying his church in his own image—a holy people who can live with a God of consuming glory (Revelation 21:1–4). Sister, the Bible will end as it begun, and that ending has already started. You testify of Christ's finished work as you joyfully live in the glory of your God today!

CONSIDER

▶ We've reached the climactic end of our journey! How does Exodus 40:34–35 capture the central purpose of Israel's redemption from Egypt?

▶ How does Exodus 40 point the reader back to God's dwelling with man at the start of Scripture (see Genesis 3:8)? How does Exodus 40 point the reader forward to a greater Tabernacle to come (see John 1:1–18)?

▶ The full experience of your redemption in Christ is ahead, and yet it has already begun! How does your enjoyment of God today testify to that truth?

BELIEVE

And I heard a loud voice from the throne saying, "Behold, the dwelling place of God is with man. He will dwell with them, and they will be his people, and God himself will be with them as their God."

REVELATION 21:3

READ

Exodus
40:1–38

IDENTIFY

Moses wrote Exodus with his eyes on his original audience, but the Divine Author spoke to instruct *you*. How is God's inspired Word guiding you to your promised home?

I love stories. My earliest years were spent in Ghana among neighbors who gathered to tell folktales in the evenings. I never lost my appetite for well-spun tales, and I have come to adore the narratives of the Old Testament for their mastery. Here's the summary of the story Moses tells:

God saw and heard captive Israel as she groaned in bitter enslavement. Yahweh remembered his covenant with their fathers—Abraham, Isaac, and Jacob—and he sent a hesitant prophet to lead them to freedom (Exodus 2–3). God redeemed Israel from Egypt with mighty acts of judgment. These were meant to reveal his nature to the Israelites, the Egyptians, and the nations of the earth (Exodus 7–15:21). In truth, God saved Israel from bondage to make himself known. He delivered his people—not just for freedom's sake, but for adoption (Exodus 19–24). God would dwell with Israel like a Father among his children. Israel grumbled and fell into idolatrous sin, yet God's mercy is most glorious when judgment is most deserved. He renewed the broken covenant, he empowered craftsmen to build his sanctuary, he sanctified priests to mediate his laws, and he came in glory to live with Israel (Exodus 32–40). Moses tells an epic story—and he does so with his attention fixed on a specific audience.

My love for stories has taught me that a skillful storyteller paints a world of characters without losing sight of the world of his audience. In fact, the better the narrator knows his audience, the better he can guide them to the treasures within his tale. In today's passage, we learn that Moses told the drama of the exodus for the instruction of an interesting audience. We get a clue from his last words in Exodus 40:36–38:

> Throughout all their journeys, whenever the cloud was taken up from over the tabernacle, the people of Israel would set out. But if the cloud was not taken up, then they did not set out till the day that it was taken up. For the cloud of the LORD was on the tabernacle by day, and fire was in it by night, in the sight of all the house of Israel throughout all their journeys.

The repeated words "throughout all their journeys" tell us that this story of God and Israel doesn't end here. It informs us of one additional detail—that this book of the Bible was finalized years *after* the events of the exodus itself. In other words, our narrator wouldn't know anything about Israel's latter journeys unless he was speaking long after this story. Friend, the drama of the exodus was captured for the *children* of the Israelites we've encountered over these weeks. God's inscribed Word was given to prepare this younger generation for the promised land (Psalm 95:7–10). Moses wrote and spoke to encourage *this* audience to trust in the God who remembers, redeems, provides, covenants, reveals, judges, restores, prepares, and dwells with his people. Moses told his story to guide a young Israel to the treasures of faith in Yahweh!

Sister, Moses wrote with his eyes on his original audience, but the Divine Author spoke to instruct *you* (1 Corinthians 10:11). The story of the exodus was inspired and inscribed to guide you to the treasures of faith in God the Father and his Son, our Redeemer. We have been saved from the bondage of sin by the shed blood of that Son. God has delivered us—not for freedom alone, but for himself. We are God's new covenant people; God presence dwells among us now, and one day, we will see him face-to-face.

Dearest Sister, God's Spirit uses God's inspired Word to guide us throughout all our journeys to a promised eternal home. Let's follow well!

CONSIDER

▶ How does Exodus 40:36–38 hint at an audience beyond the characters of this book?

▶ Read Psalm 95:7–10. How were the failings of the first generation of Israelites meant to instruct the children who would enter the promised land?

▶ How do the stories of Old Testament saints serve as an example for Christ's church today? See 1 Corinthians 10:11. Ask for grace to trust the Scriptures as your guide to an eternal home.

BELIEVE

Now these things happened to them as an example, but they were written down for our instruction, on whom the end of the ages has come.

1 CORINTHIANS 10:11

Take & Share

God's presence guided the Israelites "throughout all their journeys." This phrase clues us to Moses's first audience. Exodus was finalized years *after* the events of the drama for the children of those described within. God's Word was given to prepare this younger generation for the promised land. Sister, God's Word is offered to us for the same purpose. Scripture is our faithful guide in this wilderness journey to a better country. Do you know someone who needs to hear the story of Exodus to prepare them for the promised land? Take this book and share it!

ENDNOTES

WEEK 1

1 Sunday Oguntola, "Leah Sharibu Inspires Nigeria's Christians, Faces Execution by Boko Haram," *Christianity Today*, October 15, 2018, https://www.christianitytoday.com/news/2018/october/free-leah-sharibu-boko-haram-execution-dapchi-nigeria.html.

2 Rob Delaney, "A Heart That Works," November 27, 2022, in *Up First*, produced by National Public Radio, podcast, MP3 audio, 28:06, https://www.npr.org/2022/11/23/1139079952/a-heart-that-works.

3 Delaney, "A Heart That Works."

4 Adelaide Arthur, "Africa's naming traditions: Nine ways to name your child," *BBC*, December 30, 2016, https://www.bbc.com/news/world-africa-37912748.

WEEK 2

1 Frank White, "The Overview Effect," August 30, 2019, in *Houston, We Have a Podcast*, produced by NASA, podcast, MP3 audio, 39:44, https://www.nasa.gov/sites/default/files/atoms/audio/ep_107_overview_effect.mp3.

2 Irwyn Ince, "Destined for the Beauty of Diversity: Why We Press on for Ethnic Harmony," *Desiring God*, November 6, 2020, https://www.desiringgod.org/articles/destined-for-the-beauty-of-diversity.

3 R. C. Sproul, ed., *The Reformation Study Bible* (Sanford, FL: Reformation Trust Publishing, 2015), 111.

4 Michael D. Williams, *Far as the Curse is Found: The Covenant Story of Redemption* (Phillipsburg, NJ: P&R Publishing) 17–18.

5 Amanda Schmidt, "Seahorse Fact Sheet," Public Broadcasting Service, May 12, 2022, https://www.pbs.org/wnet/nature/blog/seahorse-fact-sheet/.

6 "The Insane Biology of: The Seahorse," Real Science, September 24, 2022, YouTube video, 17:09, https://www.youtube.com/watch?v=m7oWvPXz-9c&t=388s.

7 John Bunyan, *The Pilgrim's Progress: From This World to That Which Is to Come*, ed. C. J. Lovik (Wheaton, IL: Crossway), 213.

8 *Britannica*, s.v. "The rise and reign of Haile Selassie I (1916–74)." https://www.britannica.com/place/Ethiopia/The-rise-and-reign-of-Haile-Selassie-I-1916-74.

9 Yabibal Teklu, "Hard pressed but Not Crushed," *Christian History Magazine*, no. 109 (2014), https://christianhistoryinstitute.org/magazine/article/hard-pressed-but-not-crushed.

10 Frank Fortunato, "Singing Dangerously: How Christians Endure Persecution Through Song," [Working paper] *Global Forum on Arts and Christian Faith*, vol. 5, no. 1 (2017): 1-8.

WEEK 3

1 Abigail Beall, "How Long Can I Survive Without Water," *BBC Future*, October 19, 2020, https://www.bbc.com/future/article/20201016-why-we-cant-survive-without-water.

2 Elizabeth Loftus, "Elizabeth Loftus: How Can Our Memories Be Manipulated," October 13, 2017, in *TED Radio Hour*, produced by National Public Radio, podcast, MP3 audio, 14:44, https://www.npr.org/transcripts/557424726.

3 Daniel Yetman, "What's the Link Between Stress, Anxiety, and Vertigo," ed. Angela Bell, *Healthline*, October 8, 2020, https://www.healthline.com/health/can-stress-cause-vertigo#can-anxiety-cause-vertigo.

4 Cate Lineberry, "The Story Behind the Star-Spangled Banner: How the flag that flew proudly over Fort McHenry inspired an anthem and made its way to the Smithsonian," The *Smithsonian Magazine*, March 1, 2007, https://www.smithsonianmag.com/history/the-story-behind-the-star-spangled-banner-149220970/.

5 R. C. Sproul, ed., *The Reformation Study Bible* (Sanford, FL: Reformation Trust Publishing, 2015), 121.

6 Sproul, *The Reformation Study Bible*, 121.

7 Deepa Sukumar, "If There's a Force in Heaven, Show Yourself," September 20, 2022, in *Compelled Podcast*, produced by Paul Hastings, podcast, MP3 audio, 45:50, https://compelledpodcast.com/episodes/deepa-sukumar.

WEEK 4

1 Maris Blechner, "The Value of Words," June 24, 2015, in *The Moth Podcast*, executive produced by Sarah Austin Jenness, podcast, MP3 audio, 15:06, https://themoth.org/storytellers/maris-blechner.

2 Tim Barnett, "A Response to the Sparkle Creed," *Stand to Reason: Clear-Thinking Christianity*, August 28, 2023, https://www.str.org/w/a-response-to-the-sparkle-creed.

3 Mary Wilson Hannah, "Following Jesus Far From Home: 1 Peter 2:1 –3:12," *The Gospel Coalition*, September 8, 2016, video, 53:06, https://www.youtube.com/watch?v=6eiZUQlJL9Y.

4 R.C. Sproul, "Inner Sanctum: Fear and Trembling with R. C. Sproul," *Ligonier Ministries*, May 17, 2023, video, 25:51, https://www.youtube.com/watch?v=g7jhaaxu_RM.

WEEK 5

1 Steve Richardson, "Among the Cannibals & Headhunters," August 22, 2023, in *Compelled Podcast*, produced by Paul Hastings, podcast, MP3 audio, 48:38, https://compelledpodcast.com/episodes/steve-richardson.

2 George Albert Shepperson, "David Livingstone: Scottish Explorer and Missionary," *Britannica*, September 15, 2023, https://www.britannica.com/biography/David-Livingstone.

3 Shepperson, "David Livingston," *Britannica*.

4 Ryan Jaslow, "Scientists Regenerate Hair Cells that Enable Hearing," *Harvard Medical School: News & Research*, April 19, 2023, https://hms.harvard.edu/news/scientists-regenerate-hair-cells-enable-hearing.

5 Jaslow, "Scientists Regenerate Hair Cells that Enable Hearing."

6 R. C. Sproul, ed., *The Reformation Study Bible* (Sanford, FL: Reformation Trust Publishing, 2015), 141.

WEEK 6

1 Frederick Douglass, *Narrative of the Life of Frederick Douglass, an American Slave* (New York, NY: Penguin Books, 1982) 109-110.

2 R. C. Sproul, ed., *The Reformation Study Bible* (Sanford, FL: Reformation Trust Publishing, 2015), 142.

3 Cosette Rae, "Lying as a Means of Escaping Conflict," *re-Start*, August 28, 2013, https://www.netaddictionrecovery.com/lying-as-a-means-of-escaping-conflict.

4 Joni Eareckson Tada, "Assurances of His Presence," *Sharing Hope: Joni & Friends*, June 13, 2023, https://joniandfriendsradio.simplecast.com/episodes/assurances-of-his-presence-RiqG5mqm/transcript.

5 C. S. Lewis, *The Last Battle* (New York, NY: Macmillan Publishing Company) 173.

2 Katie Morse, "WNY Groom makes his bride's dress—and she doesn't see it until the wedding day," *ABC 7 WKBW Buffalo*, December 13, 2017, https://www.wkbw.com/news/wny-groom-makes-his-bride-s-dress-and-she-doesn-t-see-it-until-the-wedding-day.

3 Laurel Walmsley, "The father who helped his son cross the finish line at the Olympics has died," *NPR*, October 4, 2022, https://www.npr.org/2022/10/04/1126776697/jim-redmond-derek-olympics-sprinter-father-dies.

WEEK 7

1 Rund Abdelfatah and Ramtin Arablouei, "The Way Back" April 20, 2023, in *Throughline Podcast*, produced by National Public Radio, podcast, MP3 audio, 56:40, https://www.npr.org/2023/04/18/1170705584/the-way-back.

2 Lisa Endlich Heffernan, "'What Do You Do?': A Stay-at-Home-Mother's Most Dreaded Question," *The Atlantic*, July 19, 2013, https://www.theatlantic.com/sexes/archive/2013/07/what-do-you-do-a-stay-at-home-mothers-most-dreaded-question/277939/.

3 Dr. Suess, *The Foot Book* (New York: Random House Children's Books, 1996) 1-4.

4 R. C. Sproul, ed., *The Reformation Study Bible* (Sanford, FL: Reformation Trust Publishing, 2015), 1899.

5 "Stella D'oro Cookies Commercial," Johnny Sunshine, April 6, 2022, YouTube video, 0:31, https://www.youtube.com/watch?v=cNrUQoM2Rzg.

WEEK 8

1 R. C. Sproul, ed., *The Reformation Study Bible* (Sanford, FL: Reformation Trust Publishing, 2015), 153.

The Gospel Truth for Women series helps women identify their struggles, go to Scripture to meet God, and share those truths with family, friends, neighbors, and coworkers. These beautifully designed daily devotionals provide an easy-to-follow format suitable for individuals or small groups and relatable for busy women of all ages.

More from the Gospel Truth for Women series

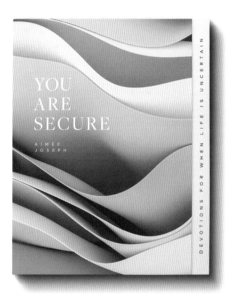

YOU ARE WELCOMED
TRISH DONOHUE

When you feel overwhelmed by life's demands, trials, and emotions, you are not alone. God welcomes you into his rest and peace when life is an unruly combination of responsibilities, relationships, interruptions, dreams, and drama. In this ten-week devotional, author and women's ministry leader Trish Donohue helps women who are weary turn to the Lord, put down their burdens, rest in his welcome, and then welcome others to walk with Jesus too.

YOU ARE SECURE
AIMEE JOSEPH

We live in a world filled with anxiety, turmoil, and constant change. We may be tempted to think that feelings of instability and insecurity are mostly modern problems, but they have plagued the human heart from the beginning. In this eight-week devotional centered on the book of Colossians, Aimee Joseph helps women see that it is their union with Christ that fills their hearts with peace. Amidst a largely insecure world, our security is anchored into the unchanging person of Jesus.